ACKNOWLEDGMENTS

Editorial Development: Kane Publishing Services
Project Manager: Richard Stull - **Editor:** Marc Gave
Design and Production: Design Five Creatives, Inc.
Cover Design: Design Five Creatives, Inc.
Production Supervisor: Sandy Batista

Photo Credits: 4: Geoff du Feu/Taxi/Getty Images. 5: Paul A. Souders/Corbis. 12: Chris Cole/Corbis. 13: Chris Trotman/Corbis. 92: David Muench/Corbis. 93: Philip Gould/Corbis. 104: Peter M. Wilson/Corbis. 106, 107: Gianni Dagli Orti/Corbis

Illustration Credits: 8, 9: Joe Boddy. 16, 17: Arthur Friedman. 96, 97: Bruce Van Patter. 100, 101: Beth Peck. 105: Molly K. Scanlon.

Text Credits: "Rain in Summer" by May Justus. Reprinted by permission of Doubleday.

Options Publishing Inc.
P.O. Box 1749
Merrimack, NH 03054-1749
TOLL FREE: 800-782-7300 FAX: 866-424-4056
www.optionspublishing.com

14 13 12 11 10 9 8 7

Test-Taking Tips

Comprehensive Reading Assessment will help you become a better reader so you can succeed in your reading tests. **First**, you will read a selection. Here is a sample paragraph from a selection.

When bathing a pet dog, you should not use shampoo that is made for people. Though these products smell sweet, they contain chemicals that can dry out or even damage a dog's skin. Many people don't realize that a dog's skin is thinner and more sensitive than human skin. When you give a dog a bath, you should use special shampoo made just for dogs. These shampoos help keep the dog's coat and skin healthy. They also make the dog's coat soft.

Next, you will answer questions about the selection. Here is a sample question. Fill in the circle of the *best* answer to this question.

1 Why should you not use shampoo made for people when you bathe a dog?

Ⓐ Dogs don't like the sweet smell of these shampoos.

Ⓑ These shampoos will not make a dog's coat soft.

Ⓒ These shampoos can damage a dog's skin.

Ⓓ You need a stronger shampoo to clean a dog.

Then, you will learn about the reading skill that the question addresses.

STRATEGIES AND TIPS Identifying Details

- **Details** help you organize the information that a writer gives you. Details give you the **5Ws and H** in a story: *who*, *what*, *when*, *where*, *why*, and *how*.

- To answer a test question about details, you do not need to reread an entire selection. You can just skim the selection until you find the detail that answers the question.

Finally, you will check your answers to help you understand why they were correct or incorrect. The following sample discusses the answer choices for this question: *Why should you not use shampoo made for people when you bathe a dog?*

Ⓐ	Dogs don't like the sweet smell of these shampoos.	**Incorrect.** The paragraph does say that these shampoos smell sweet but does not say anything about how dogs respond to the sweet smell.
Ⓑ	These shampoos will not make a dog's coat soft.	**Incorrect.** The paragraph does not discuss how shampoos made for people affect a dog's coat.
Ⓒ	These shampoos can damage a dog's skin.	**Correct.** The second sentence in the paragraph tells about this detail.
Ⓓ	You need a stronger shampoo to clean a dog.	**Incorrect.** This detail is not in the paragraph.

Try It! and **Practice** activities give you opportunities to use your understanding of the reading skills you are learning.

Strategies and Tips for Taking the Test

- Read *all* the directions at the beginning of the test. Ask your teacher to explain any directions that you do not understand.

- Carefully read each selection. Check to see if any new vocabulary words are defined.

- Read each question carefully. Be sure you know what the question is asking. Then read all the answer choices before deciding which one is correct.

- As you answer the questions, go back to the selection as often as needed.

- If you get stuck on a question, come back to it later. Answering the other questions might help you figure out the answer.

- If you are still having trouble with a question, identify the answer choices that you know are wrong. This will help you identify the correct answer.

- After you finish, check your work. Be sure that you answered every question.

Calling All Hounds

Consider two dogs. One is tall and sleek. Its sharp eyes look down over a thin, pointed nose. Its body is all muscle. In fact, you can count each rib under its powerful chest. The other dog is short and heavy, with a long body and short, stubby legs. Its droopy eyes sit within folds of flesh. Loose skin bunches down around its toes. Framing its face are long ears that hang almost to the ground.

Besides their classification as dog, what could these two animals possibly have in common? They both belong to the breed of dog called hound. What is it that makes a hound a hound? Hounds are hunting dogs, bred long ago to help people hunt prey. Hounds are classified by the type of prey they hunt, as well as by the different skills they use to hunt. There are two types of hounds—sight hounds and scent hounds.

Sight hounds, such as the smooth, lean greyhound, spot their prey from far away. Then they race after it until the chased animal becomes too exhausted to run any farther. All sight hounds **originated** in southwestern Asia. The saluki, one of the more ancient dog breeds still alive today, was first bred by **nomadic** tribes in the Middle East. The saluki is pictured on tombs of Egyptian pharaohs.

originated: came into being

nomadic: wandering

The greyhound can run at speeds of up to 37 miles per hour.

© 2004 Options Publishing, Inc.

Some other sight hounds are the longhaired Afghan hound and the Irish wolfhound, the world's tallest dog. These and other sight hounds are sleek and speedy. Sight hounds also have **keen** eyesight that allows them to spot even slight movements at a distance.

keen: excellent

On the other hand, scent hounds such as the basset hound have an extraordinary sense of smell. Like sight hounds, scent hounds also possess great **stamina**, which enables them to exhaust their prey. The most famous scent hound of all is probably the bloodhound, used by police departments to discover clues. Bloodhounds are often pictured next to fictional detectives, such as Sherlock Holmes. Why is the bloodhound such a good sniffer? Inside its nose is a membrane, or thin lining, with a surface area greater than its entire body!

stamina: the strength to withstand fatigue; endurance

Most scent hounds have features that help them chase particular prey. For example, the web-footed otterhound was used to hunt otters, animals that live primarily in water. The sturdy Rhodesian ridgeback is capable of fighting big game in Africa. Some scent hounds, such as the foxhound and the elkhound, are named for their prey.

Many scent hounds are also known for their long, droopy ears that dangle to the ground. You may think that these big ears help the dogs hear their prey as they follow its scent. However, this type of ear has nothing to do with hearing. As a scent hound runs along, nose to the ground, its ears stir the air, raising scents to its super-sensitive nose.

Though many sight hounds and scent hounds are still used for hunting, most hounds today are just plain old family companions. All hounds make wonderful pets and sometimes best friends.

The basset hound was bred to hunt rabbits and pheasants.

Go On ➡

1 **What is the author's purpose for writing this article?**

Ⓐ to describe all the different kinds of hunting dogs

Ⓑ to explain how a person can train a hunting dog

Ⓒ to persuade the reader to buy a dog

Ⓓ to inform the reader about hunting dogs known as hounds

2 **Which answer *best* fits in Circle 1?**

Ⓕ basset hound

Ⓖ Rhodesian ridgeback

Ⓗ greyhound

Ⓙ otterhound

3 **How are sight hounds different from scent hounds?**

Ⓐ Sight hounds are sleek and speedy.

Ⓑ Sight hounds have long, droopy ears.

Ⓒ Sight hounds are bred to fight big game.

Ⓓ Sight hounds have super-sensitive noses.

4 **Which of the following statements is an *opinion*?**

Ⓕ The greyhound can run as fast as 37 miles per hour.

Ⓖ All hounds make wonderful pets and sometimes best friends.

Ⓗ All sight hounds originated in southwestern Asia.

Ⓙ The saluki is pictured on tombs of Egyptian pharaohs.

5 Which detail *best* supports the idea that there are two kinds of hounds?

Ⓐ Hounds are hunting dogs, bred to help people hunt.

Ⓑ The saluki is pictured on tombs of Egyptian pharaohs.

Ⓒ Sight hounds spot their prey from far away, and scent hounds use their noses.

Ⓓ Bloodhounds are often pictured next to fictional detectives.

6 You can tell that "Calling All Hounds" is nonfiction because

Ⓕ it is a story about two dogs that become friends.

Ⓖ it is a biography about a famous hunting dog.

Ⓗ it gives information about two types of hunting dogs.

Ⓙ it is not just about one dog.

7 From the article, you can infer (guess) that greyhounds

Ⓐ corner their prey to catch them.

Ⓑ enjoy the water.

Ⓒ can run very fast.

Ⓓ are no longer used for hunting.

8 "Why is the bloodhound such a good sniffer? Inside its nose is a *membrane*, or thin lining, with a surface area greater than its entire body!" The word *membrane* means

Ⓕ a thin layer of skin.

Ⓖ an organ for thinking.

Ⓗ a very large hole.

Ⓙ a special kind of cell that helps the dog see clearly.

Directions: Read these journal entries. Then answer Questions 9–16.

Video Surprise

Friday, April 10

You may think that I'm going to write something funny in my journal today. Well, think again! I'm so angry that I can barely line up the words on the page! I am REALLY angry! Furious, boiling, fuming, irate. **LIVID**. News flash for Woody, my dear little brother (in case he has found my journal AGAIN and is reading this): Your brother Charlie is NEVER speaking to you again!

> **livid:** extremely angry; furious

Sunday, April 12

I've had two days to cool down, so I'm finally able to describe what happened last Friday. I got home late because of softball practice, and Mom was already here. "You've got mail," she said. Well, I grabbed a drink and turned on the computer. "No," Mom laughed as she handed me a letter. This was an event! I almost never get a piece of "real" mail, you know, the kind delivered by the United States Postal Service. Some people call it "snail mail." Anyway, I looked at the return address, and my eyes nearly bugged out of my head. The letter was from Hollywood, California! Even better, it was from *Video Surprise*, my favorite TV show.

I ripped open the envelope and read the first paragraph. Then I reread it.

> Dear Charlie,
> Thank you for sending us your home video, "Song to Myself." It will run during the Teen Time segment scheduled to air on May 26.

For about five seconds, I was confused. I never sent a video to *Video Surprise*. Then I figured out what had happened. "Woody!" I yelled as I tore through the house looking for my little brother.

Here's what I had quickly pieced together. A few months ago, I was in my room, listening to music. I was singing along to one of my favorite songs—I don't mind saying that I'm a pretty fair singer for a kid. Someday I'd like to sing in a rock band.

Anyway, I was posing before the mirror, using a hairbrush as a microphone. I had been dancing around and singing for a few minutes when suddenly I heard a laugh at the door. I turned around, and there was Woody with our parents' video camera! He had videotaped the whole thing! I should add that Woody likes to use our parents' video camera. They don't mind. And he's actually pretty good at it. I just don't appreciate it when I'm the subject.

Monday, April 13

I pleaded with Mom to call the television network and tell them not to run it. Did she do that? No! Instead, she said, "Charlie, why don't you take a few days to think it over? You've got such a great voice—and you'll be on national television! Besides, it's a sign of **maturity** to be able to laugh at yourself once in a while."

> **maturity:** a fully grown or developed quality

I don't mind laughing at myself. I just don't want the whole country laughing, too. Nevertheless, Mom got me thinking. Maybe I could have a *Video Surprise* party!

Thursday, April 16

Another letter came today. It congratulated me and said that the video of me, "Song to Myself," had been selected as a finalist for the $500 weekly prize! Here's the deal: They're flying our whole family (including Woody) to Hollywood for the show! But get this. Woody says that if I win the money, he should get half. Well, who knows? Hollywood . . . national TV . . . I might just be in a forgiving mood.

Go On ➡

9 **What is the theme of Charlie's journal writing?**

Ⓐ Think before you write anything down.

Ⓑ Bad things can sometimes turn out to be good things.

Ⓒ Little brothers shouldn't interfere with their big brothers.

Ⓓ Always close the door to your room.

10 **What is Charlie's main problem?**

Ⓕ Woody sneaks up on Charlie and videotapes him.

Ⓖ Charlie is too upset to handle the situation.

Ⓗ Charlie does not want *Video Surprise* to show the videotape.

Ⓙ Charlie needs to find a way to keep Woody from reading his journal.

11 **How might Charlie's journal have been different if Woody had videotaped him singing in a school talent show?**

Ⓐ The story would have been exactly the same.

Ⓑ Charlie would have been happy to have a tape of his performance.

Ⓒ Woody's parents would have done the taping, not Woody.

Ⓓ Charlie would have won the talent show.

12 **In his last journal entry, Charlie is in a forgiving mood because**

Ⓕ he is planning a *Video Surprise* party.

Ⓖ he got his first letter by "snail mail" in a long time.

Ⓗ the video wins a $500 prize.

Ⓙ the video is selected as a finalist for a $500 prize.

13 From the details in Charlie's journal, you can conclude that the TV show *Video Surprise* is

Ⓐ a mystery show.

Ⓑ a quiz show.

Ⓒ a home video show.

Ⓓ a show that previews upcoming music videos.

14 Which event happened *before* Charlie first got a letter from *Video Surprise*?

Ⓕ Woody taped Charlie singing into a hairbrush.

Ⓖ Charlie pleaded with his mother to tell the TV network not to run the tape.

Ⓗ Charlie decided that he might have a *Video Surprise* party.

Ⓙ The video "Song to Myself" ran during the Teen Time segment of *Video Surprise*.

15 Which word *best* describes Charlie's feeling toward Woody by April 16?

Ⓐ livid

Ⓑ forgiving

Ⓒ amused

Ⓓ polite

16 Which detail from Charlie's journal tells you that Woody sometimes reads it?

Ⓕ Woody likes to use his parents' video camera.

Ⓖ There is a message in the journal to Woody.

Ⓗ A letter arrives from *Video Surprise*.

Ⓙ Charlie writes an invitation to a *Video Surprise* party.

Directions: Read the article "Mia Hamm: Spotlight on Women's Sports." Then answer Questions 17–24.

Mia Hamm: Spotlight on Women's Sports

Mia Hamm plays in the 1996 Olympics.

consecutive: following one after another

poise: a state of calm or composure

On a dismal, rainy day, when many kids preferred to stay indoors, RFK Stadium in Washington, D.C. was packed with young female soccer fans. Hundreds of girls filled the stands, waiting to cheer for number 9, their soccer idol. Finally, their wait ended as Mia Hamm, the star player for the Washington Freedom, dashed onto the field.

Mia Hamm was actually much more than the star player for the Freedom. She was also the star player of the U.S. Women's National Team. Mia is probably the best all-around women's soccer player in the world.

In 1987, at the age of fifteen, Mia became the youngest player ever on the U.S. Women's National Soccer Team. Even four years later, in 1991, when the U.S. National Team won the World Championship, she was still the youngest player on the team. As a student at the University of North Carolina, she led her team to four **consecutive** national championships. Eventually, the school retired her number—19. No other University of North Carolina soccer player will wear that number.

It's not surprising to learn that Mia Hamm has had a significant impact on women's sports. Hamm's style of play, her **poise**, and her determination have set an example not only for soccer players but also for women competing in every sport. At the 1996 Atlanta Olympic Games,

Mia led the U.S. team that won the gold medal. Eighty thousand fans witnessed the final match. This attendance set a record. Never before had so many people watched a women's sporting event.

Hamm has earned the praise of her fellow athletes for her quickness, speed, and will to succeed. Those who knew Mia as a young child, however, might not have predicted her success. Hamm credits growing up as one of six siblings with developing her competitive spirit. As Hamm herself recalls, she hated losing so much that she quit many of the various games she played with her siblings. She figured that if she quit before the game was over, she couldn't really lose. Then, when Mia was seven, she discovered soccer. Suddenly, the game wasn't just about winning and losing. Soccer was all about playing the game. From that point on, Mia's passion for the game has meant giving it her all for a win.

Hamm is also respected for more than her athletic ability. Though shy and soft-spoken and not one to seek out stardom, Hamm realizes that fame has given her an opportunity to promote women's sports. That's why you'll see her at girls' sports clinics and charity games all over the world.

Mia Hamm has also organized the Mia Hamm Foundation, which has two purposes. One is to help fight bone marrow disease, which killed her brother Garrett. The other is to develop further opportunities for young women who want to participate in sports.

Mia Hamm signs autographs after a game.

As the skies eventually brightened over RFK Stadium, the huge crowd of fans applauded. The team estimated that when Mia Hamm played, she'd bring an extra 3,000 to 5,000 people to the stadium. Many of the fans were girls like the ones who hang on the rails after the game, hoping for an autograph or a chance to talk with Mia. As Hamm moved along the fence, signing her name on their programs, these fans were not disappointed.

Go On ➡

17 **What is the author's purpose for writing this article?**

Ⓐ to describe how to play soccer

Ⓑ to persuade the reader to play soccer

Ⓒ to entertain the reader with humorous stories about soccer

Ⓓ to give readers information about Mia Hamm and her life

18 **Mia often quit the games she played with her siblings because**

Ⓕ she got tired of playing.

Ⓖ they were too competitive.

Ⓗ she hated losing.

Ⓙ the games did not involve quickness and speed.

19 **Which answer *best* fits in Circle 1?**

Ⓐ speedy

Ⓑ nervous

Ⓒ friendly

Ⓓ famous

20 **Unlike the way Mia felt about games with her siblings, she now**

Ⓕ feels passion for the game of soccer.

Ⓖ always worries about losing in games.

Ⓗ often quits before the game is over.

Ⓙ doesn't really care if she wins or not.

© 2004 Options Publishing, Inc.

21 **Which statement is an *opinion*?**

Ⓐ No other University of North Carolina soccer player will wear that number.

Ⓑ Hamm credits growing up as one of six siblings with developing her competitive spirit.

Ⓒ When Mia Hamm plays, she brings an extra 3,000 to 5,000 people to the stadium.

Ⓓ She is probably the best women's soccer player in the world.

22 **Which detail supports the idea that Mia Hamm has had a significant impact on women's sports?**

Ⓕ Those who knew Mia as a young child, however, might not have predicted her success.

Ⓖ Hamm is also respected for more than her athletic ability.

Ⓗ Soccer was all about playing the game.

Ⓙ Never had so many people watched a women's sports event.

23 **From the article, you can infer, or guess, that Mia Hamm**

Ⓐ hates playing games with her siblings.

Ⓑ likes to be on TV.

Ⓒ gets tired of meeting her fans.

Ⓓ is generous with her time and money.

24 **Which of the following events happened *first* in Mia's life?**

Ⓕ Mia played for the Washington Freedom.

Ⓖ Mia played soccer at the 1991 World Championships.

Ⓗ Mia became a member of the U.S. National Soccer Team.

Ⓙ Mia played soccer at the University of North Carolina.

Directions: Read this Spanish folktale. Then answer Questions 25–32.

Medio-Pollito's Bad Luck

tortilla
(tor-TEE-yuh):
a round, flat bread
rolled out into the
shape of a pancake

adios
(ah-dee-OHSS):
the Spanish word
meaning "goodbye"

Long ago, a fine black hen waited for her brood to hatch. The first several chicks to hatch were plump, but the last one was a sight to behold! He was as flat as a **tortilla**, with one eye, one leg, one ear, and one pitiful wing. His mother named him Medio-Pollito (MAY-dee-oh poh-YEE-toh), which in Spanish means "half-chick."

The other chicks were well-behaved and stuck close to the farmyard, pecking for grubs in the dirt. But Medio-Pollito was not content to stay by his mother's side. He wanted to travel to see the king. One day, without so much as an **adios** to his dear Mama, Medio-Pollito hopped down the dusty road.

Soon he came to a river. "Medio-Pollito," called Water, "please come and help me. A log has fallen across my middle, and I am rising over my banks."

"I'm too busy to stop," laughed Medio-Pollito. "I'm on my way to see the king!"

The chick hopped along the road. Soon he passed a campfire smoldering on the ground.

"Medio-Pollito," called out Fire, "please feed me some sticks quickly or I shall go out!"

But Medio-Pollito hopped on without a pause. "I have more important things to do," he called over his narrow shoulder.

Not long after, Medio-Pollito passed a tall tree with a large wind caught in its branches. "Please, Medio-Pollito," implored Wind, "I am all tangled up, and I must continue to blow north. Won't you help me?" The half-chick hopped on his way, too hurried to lend a hand.

Soon he arrived at the palace gate. "Half a chicken!" exclaimed a man, grabbing the chick. It was the chef, preparing soup for the king's dinner. He plopped the chick right into a soup pot filled with water.

"Water," begged Medio-Pollito, "please save me!"

"I once asked you for help," Water responded. "I cannot help you now."

The chef carried the pot to the fire. "Please, Fire, help me!" squawked the half-chick.

Fire answered hotly, "You were in such a hurry before that you would not stop for me. Now **fend** for yourself."

fend: get along without help

Medio-Pollito hopped up and down in the boiling broth. He managed to escape from the soup, only to scorch his wing on the flames. Since the chick was no longer good for soup, the chef picked up the bird with the blackened wing and tossed him out the window.

Medio-Pollito hopped away, thinking that he was free. Just then, however, Wind blew by, scooped up Medio-Pollito, and dropped him on the highest rooftop. There he remains to this very day—a weather vane—pointing out which direction Wind blows.

Go On ➡

25 Which event happened just *after* Medio-Pollito left home?

Ⓐ Medio-Pollito came to a fire smoldering on the ground.

Ⓑ The chef at the palace plopped Medio-Pollito into a soup pot.

Ⓒ Medio-Pollito came to a tree with the wind caught in its branches.

Ⓓ Medio-Pollito came to a river that was going to flood its banks.

26 Which detail tells you how Medio-Pollito got his name?

Ⓕ Medio-Pollito hopped up and down in the boiling broth.

Ⓖ Wind dropped Medio-Pollito on the highest rooftop.

Ⓗ Medio-Pollito was as flat as a tortilla, with one eye, one leg, one ear, and one pitiful wing.

Ⓙ Medio-Pollito was not content to stay by his mother's side.

27 What unexpected event occurs when Medio-Pollito arrives at the palace?

Ⓐ He becomes a weather vane.

Ⓑ He argues with the chef.

Ⓒ He does not stop to help the fire.

Ⓓ The chef grabs him and drops him into the soup.

28 What is the theme of this story?

Ⓕ Goodness overcomes evil.

Ⓖ If you are determined and work hard, you will succeed.

Ⓗ If you do not help others, they may not help you when you need them.

Ⓙ Prepare before starting a long journey.

29 How can you tell that "Medio-Pollito's Bad Luck" is a folktale?

Ⓐ It is about real events that happen to real people.

Ⓑ It is a story that has talking animals and teaches a lesson.

Ⓒ It takes place in the future.

Ⓓ It is about chickens.

30 Which word *best* describes Medio-Pollito's feelings toward Fire, Water, and Wind?

Ⓕ courageous

Ⓖ helpful

Ⓗ uncaring

Ⓙ concerned

31 From the details in the story, what conclusion can you draw about Wind?

Ⓐ Wind blows Medio-Pollito up to the rooftop to punish him.

Ⓑ Wind likes Medio-Pollito and wants to help him.

Ⓒ Wind blows out the fire under the soup pot to save Medio-Pollito.

Ⓓ Wind wants to teach Medio-Pollito how to fly.

32 "He managed to escape from the soup, only to *scorch* his wing on the flames." What does the word *scorch* mean?

Ⓕ to dry

Ⓖ to warm

Ⓗ to burn

Ⓙ to get wet

STOP

Directions: Read the article "Calling All Hounds" again. Then compare your answers with the answers given here.

Calling All Hounds

Consider two dogs. One is tall and sleek. Its sharp eyes look down over a thin, pointed nose. Its body is all muscle. In fact, you can count each rib under its powerful chest. The other dog is short and heavy, with a long body and short, stubby legs. Its droopy eyes sit within folds of flesh. Loose skin bunches down around its toes. Framing its face are long ears that hang almost to the ground.

Besides their classification as dog, what could these two animals possibly have in common? They both belong to the breed of dog called hound. What is it that makes a hound a hound? Hounds are hunting dogs, bred long ago to help people hunt prey. Hounds are classified by the type of prey they hunt, as well as by the different skills they use to hunt. There are two types of hounds—sight hounds and scent hounds.

Sight hounds, such as the smooth, lean greyhound, spot their prey from far away. Then they race after it until the chased animal becomes too exhausted to run any farther. All sight hounds **originated** in southwestern Asia. The saluki, one of the more ancient dog breeds still alive today, was first bred by **nomadic** tribes in the Middle East. The saluki is pictured on tombs of Egyptian pharaohs.

originated: came into being

nomadic: wandering

The greyhound can run at speeds of up to 37 miles per hour.

© 2004 Options Publishing, Inc.

Some other sight hounds are the longhaired Afghan hound and the Irish wolfhound, the world's tallest dog. These and other sight hounds are sleek and speedy. Sight hounds also have **keen** eyesight that allows them to spot even slight movements at a distance.

keen: excellent

On the other hand, scent hounds such as the basset hound have an extraordinary sense of smell. Like sight hounds, scent hounds also possess great **stamina**, which enables them to exhaust their prey. The most famous scent hound of all is probably the bloodhound, used by police departments to discover clues. Bloodhounds are often pictured next to fictional detectives, such as Sherlock Holmes. Why is the bloodhound such a good sniffer? Inside its nose is a membrane, or thin lining, with a surface area greater than its entire body!

stamina: the strength to withstand fatigue; endurance

Most scent hounds have features that help them chase particular prey. For example, the web-footed otterhound was used to hunt otters, animals that live primarily in water. The sturdy Rhodesian ridgeback is capable of fighting big game in Africa. Some scent hounds, such as the foxhound and the elkhound, are named for their prey.

Many scent hounds are also known for their long, droopy ears that dangle to the ground. You may think that these big ears help the dogs hear their prey as they follow its scent. However, this type of ear has nothing to do with hearing. As a scent hound runs along, nose to the ground, its ears stir the air, raising scents to its super-sensitive nose.

Though many sight hounds and scent hounds are still used for hunting, most hounds today are just plain old family companions. All hounds make wonderful pets and sometimes best friends.

The basset hound was bred to hunt rabbits and pheasants.

A

Go On ➡

Question 1 This question is about **identifying the author's purpose**.

STRATEGIES AND TIPS   Identifying Author's Purpose

- The **author's purpose** is the reason an author has for writing. The purpose can be to *entertain, persuade, inform, explain,* or *describe* something or someone to the reader. In the article "Calling All Hounds," the author wants to inform you by giving facts about two different kinds of hounds.

- Knowing the author's purpose for writing can help you better understand what you are reading.

1 **What is the author's purpose for writing this article?**

Ⓐ to describe all the different kinds of hunting dogs | **Incorrect.** The author describes only two kinds of hunting dogs in detail.

Ⓑ to explain how a person can train a hunting dog | **Incorrect.** The author does not explain how to train a hunting dog.

Ⓒ to persuade the reader to buy a dog | **Incorrect.** The article does not try to persuade the reader to buy a dog.

Ⓓ to inform the reader about hunting dogs known as hounds | **Correct.** This is the author's main purpose. The author includes information about two kinds of hounds.

TRY IT! Think about the author's purpose for writing this article. Skim the article to find three facts about hounds and write them on the lines below.

1. _____

2. _____

3. _____

PRACTICE Identifying Author's Purpose

An **author's purpose** for writing may be to *entertain, persuade, inform, explain,* or *describe*. An author may have more than one purpose for writing. Knowing the author's purpose for writing can help you better understand what you are reading.

Read each paragraph below. Think about what the author's main purpose might be. Write it on the line. Then write one detail from the paragraph to support your answer.

1. Did you ever wonder why a Dalmatian dog is the mascot of fire departments? Dalmatians were bred to be coach dogs. They ran ahead of horse-drawn coaches to chase cows and other animals out of the way. Firemen needed to get to the scene of a fire in a hurry. So, years ago, Dalmatians ran ahead of the fire wagons to chase animals—and sometimes people—out of the way.

   Purpose: _____

   Detail: _____

   _____

2. Here are some tips for giving your dog a bath: First, make sure that everything within a radius of about 10 yards is waterproof. Next, wear clothes you don't mind getting wet. Gather all of your dog's bath supplies ahead of time: shampoo, brush, comb, and hose. Don't forget the towels! Make sure there is another person to hold your dog or that there is a place where you can secure its leash. Turn on the water to a comfortable temperature—for you and your dog. Wear earplugs if you can't stand loud barking!

   Purpose: _____

   Detail: _____

   _____

A

(**STRATEGIES AND TIPS**) **Classifying**

- **Classifying** is grouping similar things together. When you read an article, you should be able to classify, or group together, similar ideas that go with the topic. For example, if the topic of an article is "hunting dogs," you might look for information in the article about the kinds of dogs that hunt, such as salukis, bloodhounds, greyhounds, and so on. These can be grouped together, or classified, as hunting dogs.

- The items that you classify may appear in several parts of an article. You may want to use a chart or an outline to keep track of similar objects or ideas.

2 **Which answer *best* fits in Circle 1?**

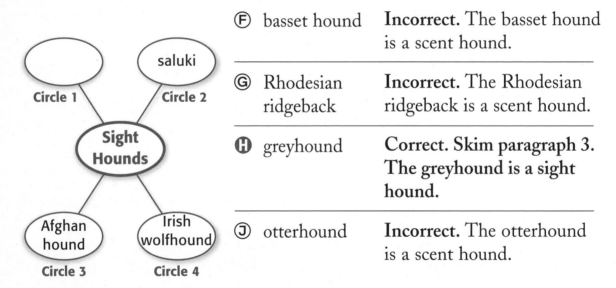

F basset hound   **Incorrect.** The basset hound is a scent hound.

G Rhodesian ridgeback   **Incorrect.** The Rhodesian ridgeback is a scent hound.

H greyhound   **Correct.** Skim paragraph 3. The greyhound is a sight hound.

J otterhound   **Incorrect.** The otterhound is a scent hound.

(**TRY IT!**) **List three characteristics of scent hounds.**

1. _____

2. _____

3. _____

A

To **classify**, you group objects or ideas that are similar. You can better understand a topic if you can classify ideas and information about that topic.

Read the following article. Think about the topic of the article.

> If your family has a dog, you may think of it as your pet—or "animal companion." You expect it to greet you when you come home and to be loving and loyal. You might train your dog to catch a ball or fetch the newspaper. But you probably don't think of it as having a real job.
>
> Many dogs, however, do work. Collies, for example, are herding dogs. They protect flocks of sheep and other farm animals. German shepherds are often trained as police dogs. They help the police force to protect homes and businesses—and people. Beagles and other dogs with a strong sense of smell work at airports, sniffing out dangerous goods brought into the country on planes.
>
> Labrador and golden retrievers often make smart and caring guide dogs. These dogs help guide blind people as they travel in a city or a town.

State the topic of the article by completing the first line below. Then list examples of the topic.

Topic: _____

1. _____

2. _____

3. _____

4. _____

Question 3 This question is about **comparing and contrasting**.

STRATEGIES AND TIPS Comparing and Contrasting

- **Comparing** is finding ways that things are alike. **Contrasting** is finding ways that things are different. Comparing and contrasting as you read can help you better understand an article.

- Sometimes you can find clue words that tell you things are being compared, such as *alike, same, both,* and *similarly*. In "Calling All Hounds," the author compares two kinds of dogs that are both hounds. Clue words that signal contrast include *unlike, on the other hand, however,* and *different*.

3 How are sight hounds different from scent hounds?

Ⓐ Sight hounds are sleek and speedy.

Correct. Read paragraph 3. It states, "These and other sight hounds are sleek and speedy."

Ⓑ Sight hounds have long, droopy ears.

Incorrect. Sight hounds do not have long, droopy ears.

Ⓒ Sight hounds are bred to fight big game.

Incorrect. Sight hounds are not bred to fight big game.

Ⓓ Sight hounds have super-sensitive noses.

Incorrect. Scent hounds, not sight hounds, have super-sensitive noses.

TRY IT! Skim the article to find information on the two kinds of hounds. Compare sight hounds with scent hounds by describing two ways they are alike. Contrast them by describing two ways they are different.

Compare: _____

_____

Contrast: _____

_____

PRACTICE Comparing and Contrasting

When authors **compare** people, events, things, or ideas, they describe how they are alike. When comparing, authors may use words such as *alike, same, both,* and *similarly*. When authors **contrast** people, events, things, or ideas, they describe how they are different. When contrasting, authors may use words such as *but, however, on the other hand,* and *different*.

Read each sentence. Circle the word or words that signal comparing or contrasting. The first one is done for you.

1. (Both) collies and Old English sheepdogs are herding dogs.

2. Portuguese water dogs work on boats, just like Newfoundlands.

3. Golden retrievers have long, silky hair. Labrador retrievers, however, have short, stubby hair.

4. Cocker spaniels are good pets for small city apartments. Similarly, Yorkshire terriers are good pets for small spaces.

Read the paragraph. Then list how collies and pulis are alike and different.

Collies and pulis are both herding dogs. Both dogs weigh about 35 pounds. Collies have long, silky hair that is white and brown. Pulis have long hair too, but it is curly and black. Collies herd sheep by running and barking. Pulis have a different method. They jump on the back of the lead sheep and nip it behind the ears to make the animal turn.

How They Are Alike: _____

_____

_____

How They Are Different: _____

_____

_____

A

STRATEGIES AND TIPS Identifying Fact and Opinion

- A **fact** is a statement that can be proved by checking in reference books, such as atlases and encyclopedias, or other sources. *Greyhounds were bred to be hunting dogs*. This is a fact that you can check in a book about dogs.

- An **opinion** is a statement that expresses what someone feels or thinks. It cannot be proved or disproved. *Greyhounds are the best hunting dogs*. This is one person's opinion. Another person might think differently.

4 **Which of the following statements is an *opinion*?**

Ⓕ	The greyhound can run as fast as 37 miles per hour.	**Incorrect.** This is a fact from the caption for the picture on page 4.
Ⓖ	All hounds make wonderful pets and sometimes best friends.	**Correct. This is an opinion. Many hounds make good pets, but no one knows for sure if *all* hounds make good pets.**
Ⓗ	All sight hounds originated in southwestern Asia.	**Incorrect.** This is a fact. It could be checked in a reference source.
Ⓙ	The saluki is pictured on tombs of Egyptian pharaohs.	**Incorrect.** This is a fact that is stated in paragraph 3.

TRY IT! **Write *F* for fact or *O* for opinion before each statement below.**

1. _____ The bloodhound is probably the best scent hound.

2. _____ Sight hounds can spot their prey from far away.

3. _____ Sight hounds and scent hounds are described in this article.

INSTRUCTION FOR CALLING ALL HOUNDS

A

A **fact** can be proved; an **opinion** cannot. An opinion is what someone feels or thinks. If you can recognize the difference between a fact and an opinion, you can better understand what you read.

Read the ad below. Look for facts and opinions as you read. Then write three facts and three opinions from the ad in the chart below.

Everyone Needs the Handy Dandy Tool!

The Handy Dandy is made of steel with a rubber grip handle. It has a screwdriver, hammer, wire cutter, and pliers—all in one! It is fun and easy to use. A handy clip lets you hook it onto your belt. You will never be without the tools you need again! Buy the Handy Dandy Tool—you won't be sorry. It costs just $29.95.

Facts	Opinions
1.	1.
2.	2.
3.	3.

A

Question 5 This question is about **identifying supporting details**.

STRATEGIES AND TIPS Identifying Supporting Details

- **Supporting details** support, or build on, the main idea. Without supporting details, the main idea can be difficult to understand. For example, the main idea of "Calling All Hounds" is that hunting dogs known as hounds can be classified as scent hounds and sight hounds. The author supports this idea by giving examples of both kinds of hounds.

- Not all details support the main idea. Some details give information about other things, people, or places mentioned in the article. Though these details may be interesting, they do not necessarily support the main idea.

5 **Which detail *best* supports the idea that there are two kinds of hounds?**

Ⓐ Hounds are hunting dogs, bred to help people hunt.

Incorrect. This detail tells about hounds in general, not the two different kinds.

Ⓑ The saluki is pictured on tombs of Egyptian pharaohs.

Incorrect. This is an interesting detail, but it does not support the main idea.

Ⓒ Sight hounds spot their prey from far away, and scent hounds use their noses.

Correct. These details help the reader understand the main idea.

Ⓓ Bloodhounds are often pictured next to fictional detectives.

Incorrect. This detail does not help the reader understand the differences between the two kinds of hounds.

TRY IT! Look for details in the article that help you understand the main idea. Then answer the questions below.

1. How do a scent hound's ears help it smell well?

_____

2. How do sight hounds catch their prey?

_____

 **PRACTICE** Identifying Supporting Details

Supporting details support, or build on, the main idea. They help the reader understand the main idea.

Read the following short article about the Arctic fox. Look for details that support the main idea.

> The Arctic fox is a member of the dog family. This small, white fox lives in the Arctic region, which has an extremely cold climate. The Arctic fox is a crafty hunter. It often follows polar bears. After a polar bear kills its prey and eats its fill, the little fox moves in to eat the leftovers.
>
> Many birds go to the Arctic in spring to build nests on the high cliffs. Arctic foxes are ready to steal eggs or snatch a baby bird that falls from its nest. The fox will eat some of the eggs and birds, but it will put others "in storage" underground for the lean winter months, when there is nothing to eat.

The main idea is given below. Fill in the chart with supporting details that build on the main idea. The first one has been done for you.

Main Idea:	The Arctic fox is a crafty hunter.
Detail:	After a polar bear kills its prey and eats its fill, the little fox moves in to eat the leftovers.
Detail:	
Detail:	

Question 6 This question is about **identifying genre.**

STRATEGIES AND TIPS Identifying Genre

- **Genre** is the type of literature you read, such as *stories, poetry,* or *informational articles.*

- *Fiction* is writing that tells about characters, places, and events that are not real. *Myths, folktales, fables, tall tales,* and *short stories* are fiction genres.

- *Nonfiction* is writing that gives you facts about real people, places, events, and things. *Articles, essays, biographies,* and *autobiographies* are nonfiction genres. The author of "Calling All Hounds" provided facts in the article about two types of hunting dogs.

6 **You can tell that "Calling All Hounds" is nonfiction because**

Ⓕ it is a story about two dogs that become friends.	**Incorrect.** It is not a story.
Ⓖ it is a biography about a famous hunting dog.	**Incorrect.** It is not a biography about a famous dog.
Ⓗ it gives information about two types of hunting dogs.	**Correct. The article gives facts about sight hounds and scent hounds.**
Ⓙ it is not just about one dog.	**Incorrect.** This answer is true, but it does not tell why the article is nonfiction.

TRY IT! **Skim "Calling All Hounds." Find two other details that would classify this article as nonfiction. Write them below.**

1. _____

_____

2. _____

_____

A

> **Genre** is the type of literature you read. *Nonfiction* includes *biographies* and *informational articles* about real people, places, events, and things. *Fiction* includes *stories* about made-up people, places, events, and things.

Read each paragraph below. Decide whether it is *fiction* or *nonfiction*. Circle your answer. Then give a reason why you made that choice.

1. Penguins are birds that live in the waters that surround Antarctica. Although they cannot fly, penguins are very good swimmers. A layer of fat and three layers of waterproof feathers keep a penguin warm and dry in the icy-cold water.

    fiction   nonfiction

    Reason: _____

2. In the early 1900s, buildings in New York City were no more than four or five stories tall. The introduction of electricity changed that. With electricity, people could run elevators. In 1923, the first "skyscraper" was built on a triangular-shaped piece of ground in New York City. It was called the Flatiron Building, because its shape resembled an iron.

    fiction   nonfiction

    Reason: _____

3. Tony Chavez was having a bad day. He was looking over his book report as he walked to school. The wind blew it from his hands. It landed in a tree. When Tony climbed the tree to get it, his pants ripped. "What next?" he asked himself. He didn't notice that he was just above a huge puddle of water.

    fiction   nonfiction

    Reason: _____

INSTRUCTION FOR CALLING ALL HOUNDS

A

INSTRUCTION FOR CALLING ALL HOUNDS

STRATEGIES AND TIPS **Making Inferences**

- One way to gain meaning from what you read is to **make inferences,** or logical guesses. You make an inference by using the information in an article, along with your own knowledge and common sense.

- Use the information and what you already know to make an inference. From the information in "Calling All Hounds," you could infer (make a guess) that a scent hound might be helpful in locating a person who was lost.

7 **From the article, you can infer (guess) that greyhounds**

Ⓐ corner their prey to catch them.   **Incorrect.** There are no details in the article to suggest that greyhounds corner their prey.

Ⓑ enjoy the water.   **Incorrect.** This may be true, but you can't infer it from the article.

Ⓒ can run very fast.   **Correct.** Greyhounds can run as fast as 37 miles per hour. Using what you know about car speed, you can infer that greyhounds run very fast.

Ⓓ are no longer used for hunting.   **Incorrect.** There are no details in the article that help you infer this.

TRY IT! **List two details from the article that support this inference:** *Being short and stocky is a good characteristic for a scent hound to have.*

1. _____

2. _____

An author does not always give you all the information about a topic directly. You may need to find clues in an article and then make your own **inferences,** or logical guesses, about the topic. When you make inferences, you use these clues and your own knowledge and common sense.

Read this paragraph about armadillos.

> Armadillos are small mammals that live in the American Southwest. These unusual-looking animals have thick, bony plates growing out of their skin. In addition, some armadillos have sharp, spiny hair growing from between their plates. This armor serves the armadillo well. When an enemy approaches, the armadillo curls up into a ball. The enemy is unable to attack. When an enemy comes, the armadillo can also burrow into the ground. Its armor blocks the entrance to the burrow and protects the armadillo.

Circle the inference you can make based on the details in the paragraph. Then write three details that support your inference.

Armadillos fight off their predators.

Armadillos are well-protected against their enemies.

Detail 1: _____

_____

Detail 2: _____

_____

Detail 3: _____

_____

INSTRUCTION FOR CALLING ALL HOUNDS

A

Question 8 This question is about **using context clues**.

STRATEGIES AND TIPS Using Context Clues

- **Context clues** are the words, phrases, or sentences around an unfamiliar word.

- Unfamiliar words can also be defined with a definition clue. Read this sentence: "Sight hounds also have <u>keen</u> eyesight that <u>allows them to spot even slight movements at a distance</u>." Other words in the sentence help you understand that keen means "sharp or sensitive."

- Try substituting the different answer choices for the unfamiliar word in the test sentence. This can sometimes help you find the answer that makes sense.

---

8 "Why is the bloodhound such a good sniffer? Inside its nose is a *membrane*, or thin lining, with a surface area greater than its entire body!" The word *membrane* means

F	a thin layer of skin.	**Correct.** The author helps define the word with the phrase "thin lining."
G	an organ for thinking.	**Incorrect.** This is not the definition given.
H	a very large hole.	**Incorrect.** This is not the definition given.
J	a special kind of cell that helps the dog see clearly.	**Incorrect.** The sentence is about smelling, not seeing.

TRY IT! Circle the context clues in each sentence that help you understand each underlined word.

1. Hounds help people hunt <u>prey</u>, such as rabbits, deer, and foxes.

2. Hounds race after their prey until it becomes too <u>exhausted</u> to run any more.

3. The <u>sturdy</u> Rhodesian ridgeback is capable of fighting big game in Africa.

© 2004 Options Publishing, Inc.

A

PRACTICE Using Context Clues

Context clues are the words and phrases that can be found in sentences surrounding an unfamiliar word. These clues can help you figure out the meaning of the unfamiliar word.

Read the following pairs of sentences. Circle the clue that helps you understand the meaning of the underlined word. Then write a sentence using the word.

1. Jeremy was <u>confused</u>. "I'm puzzled about the homework," he said.

    _____

    _____

2. The workers placed an additional layer of bricks to <u>fortify</u> the wall. They hoped their plan would make the wall stronger.

    _____

    _____

3. I wanted to <u>communicate</u> to Mom that I'd be late getting home. I had to find a way to contact her.

    _____

    _____

4. Rita spent an hour a day <u>instructing</u> her dog. She taught him a number of useful things.

    _____

    _____

5. Rajiv <u>sampled</u> many unfamiliar foods at the party. He tried a little bit of everything.

    _____

    _____

INSTRUCTION FOR CALLING ALL HOUNDS

A

Video Surprise

Friday, April 10

You may think that I'm going to write something funny in my journal today. Well, think again! I'm so angry that I can barely line up the words on the page! I am REALLY angry! Furious, boiling, fuming, irate. **LIVID**. News flash for Woody, my dear little brother (in case he has found my journal AGAIN and is reading this): Your brother Charlie is NEVER speaking to you again!

livid: extremely angry; furious

Sunday, April 12

I've had two days to cool down, so I'm finally able to describe what happened last Friday. I got home late because of softball practice, and Mom was already here. "You've got mail," she said. Well, I grabbed a drink and turned on the computer. "No," Mom laughed as she handed me a letter. This was an event! I almost never get a piece of "real" mail, you know, the kind delivered by the United States Postal Service. Some people call it "snail mail." Anyway, I looked at the return address, and my eyes nearly bugged out of my head. The letter was from Hollywood, California!

Even better, it was from *Video Surprise*, my favorite TV show.

I ripped open the envelope and read the first paragraph. Then I reread it.

Dear Charlie,

Thank you for sending us your home video, "Song to Myself." It will run during the Teen Time segment scheduled to air on May 26.

For about five seconds, I was confused. I never sent a video to *Video Surprise*. Then I figured out what had happened. "Woody!" I yelled as I tore through the house looking for my little brother.

Here's what I had quickly pieced together. A few months ago, I was in my room, listening to music. I was singing along to one of my favorite songs—I don't mind saying that I'm a pretty fair singer for a kid. Some day I'd like to sing in a rock band.

Anyway, I was posing before the mirror, using a hairbrush as a microphone. I had been dancing around and singing for a few minutes when suddenly I heard a laugh at the door. I turned around, and there was Woody with our parents' video camera! He had videotaped the whole thing! I should add that Woody likes to use our parents' video camera. They don't mind. And he's actually pretty good at it. I just don't appreciate it when I'm the subject.

Monday, April 13

I pleaded with Mom to call the television network and tell them not to run it. Did she do that? No! Instead, she said, "Charlie, why don't you take a few days to think it over? You've got such a great voice—and you'll be on national television! Besides, it's a sign of **maturity** to be able to laugh at yourself once in a while."

I don't mind laughing at myself. I just don't want the whole country laughing, too. Nevertheless, Mom got me thinking. Maybe I could have a *Video Surprise* party!

> **maturity:** a fully grown or developed quality

Thursday, April 16

Another letter came today. It congratulated me and said that the video of me, "Song to Myself," had been selected as a finalist for the $500 weekly prize! Here's the deal: They're flying our whole family (including Woody) to Hollywood for the show! But get this. Woody says that if I win the money, he should get half. Well, who knows? Hollywood . . . national TV . . . I might just be in a forgiving mood.

Go On ➡

A

Question 9 This question is about **understanding theme**.

STRATEGIES AND TIPS Understanding Theme

- The **theme** is the message of a story. The theme sometimes relates to a lesson the main character learns or does not learn. Be careful not to confuse the theme of a story with its topic. The topic refers to what the writing is about. The theme is the message or point the writer makes.

- When identifying a theme, think about important events that occur. What was the main character like at the beginning of the story? What was the character like at the end? What lesson did he or she learn?

9 **What is the theme of Charlie's journal writing?**

Ⓐ	Think before you write anything down.	**Incorrect.** Charlie thinks that Woody reads his journal, but this is not the message of the story.
Ⓑ	Bad things can sometimes turn out to be good things.	**Correct.** Charlie changes his mind when he learns that the tape could win a prize and that his family may go to Hollywood.
Ⓒ	Little brothers shouldn't interfere with their big brothers.	**Incorrect.** At first, Charlie is angry with Woody, but this is not the main message of his journal.
Ⓓ	Always close the door to your room.	**Incorrect.** This is not the lesson Charlie learns.

TRY IT! Find three details in the journal that support this theme: *Bad things can sometimes turn out to be good things.*

1. _____

2. _____

3. _____

PRACTICE • Understanding Theme

The **theme** is the message or lesson in a piece of writing.

Read the following story. As you read, think about the theme.

Chris had always wanted to be in the school play. This year she heard it was going to be a musical. Chris was a good singer, but her dancing wasn't so great. Her mom and her grandfather were both good dancers, but not Chris. "I've got to get a part in that play," she thought. "Maybe Grandpa can help me when he visits tonight."

That night, Chris asked Grandpa to help her. "Sure," he said. "I'll put on some records, and we'll see how it goes." Chris's face fell. "Uh oh, a record," she thought. "He still plays records, not CDs. He'll probably teach me the waltz!"

Sure enough, Chris's grandfather taught her dances that were popular when he was her age. She was upset, but she didn't want to hurt his feelings. Besides, Chris enjoyed learning the old steps. And she was getting pretty good. "I guess I won't make the play," she thought. "But I can do a mean fox trot!"

On the day of the tryouts, Chris went to watch. She knew she couldn't try out because she didn't know any of the new dance steps. Mr. Goodman, the play's director, got up on to the stage. "This play is set in the 1940s," he said. "So the singing and dancing will be from that time. Does anyone know the fox trot or the lindy hop?"

Chris almost jumped out of her skin. Those were the very dances that Grandpa had taught her to do!

On the lines below, write the theme of the story.

_____

_____

INSTRUCTION FOR VIDEO SURPRISE

A

Question 10 This question is about **understanding plot**.

Understanding Plot

- **Plot** is what happens in a story. The important events make up the plot, and the final event is the *outcome*. Sometimes the plot involves a problem or conflict that a main character must resolve. In this story, Woody creates a problem for Charlie. The problem solves itself, however, without any help from Charlie or Woody.

- Understanding important events in a story can help you understand other story elements, such as character, setting, and theme.

10 What is Charlie's main problem?

⒡ Woody sneaks up on Charlie and videotapes him.	**Incorrect.** The fact that Woody sneaks up on Charlie and videotapes him is the cause of the problem. It is not the main problem.
⒢ Charlie is too upset to handle the situation.	**Incorrect.** Charlie is upset, but it is not his main problem.
⒣ Charlie does not want *Video Surprise* to show the videotape.	**Correct.** Charlie is afraid that everyone will laugh at him if the tape is shown on TV. He wants to find a way to stop the show from showing it.
⒥ Charlie needs to find a way to keep Woody from reading his journal.	**Incorrect.** Charlie is annoyed that Woody reads his journal, but his main problem is that Woody sent the video to *Video Surprise*.

TRY IT! At first, Charlie wants to stop Woody's video from being shown on TV. But by his last journal entry, Charlie is not upset anymore. What two events change Charlie's mind?

1. _____

2. _____

PRACTICE **Understanding Plot**

The **plot** is what happens in a story. It often includes a problem that the main character tries to resolve.

Read the story below. Then answer the questions.

> Mandy opened the envelope and read the invitation inside. "Wow!" she cried. "I've been invited to a costume party. That's great!" When Mandy looked more closely at the invitation, her face dropped. "Oh! The party is tonight," she moaned. "My invitation must have been lost in the mail! I want to go, but I don't have a costume."
>
> Mandy was miserable. "I can't come up with a costume in a couple of hours," she thought. "I might as well just sit on the front porch and watch the cars go by. I can't go."
>
> Mandy sat on her porch. She stared at the black road. She watched the cars go back and forth on either side of the white stripe in the middle of the road. Suddenly, Mandy had an idea! She ran into the house, got the adhesive tape, and ran into her room. About an hour later, she came out in her costume. "I'm ready to go to the party," she announced.
>
> Mandy was wearing black pants, a black turtleneck shirt, and black gloves. Down the center of her shirt and pants was a stripe made out of white tape. "I'm Route 66," she said. "I'm the old highway to California!"

1. What is the problem?

_____

2. What is the solution?

_____

_____

A

INSTRUCTION FOR VIDEO SURPRISE

STRATEGIES AND TIPS Identifying Setting

- The **setting** of a story is where and when the events of a story happen. The setting often affects what happens in the story. For example, if Charlie lived in Los Angeles, winning a trip to Hollywood might not seem so wonderful.

- When you read, ask yourself: *Where do the events take place? When do these events happen? How does the setting affect what happens?*

11 How might Charlie's journal have been different if Woody had videotaped him singing in a school talent show?

Ⓐ The story would have been exactly the same.

Incorrect. Because Charlie's performance would have been planned, the plot would probably have developed differently.

Ⓑ Charlie would have been happy to have a tape of his performance.

Correct. Charlie is angry because Woody taped him without his knowing it. Charlie might have liked watching a tape of his talent show performance.

Ⓒ Woody's parents would have done the taping, not Woody.

Incorrect. There is no reason to assume this, since Woody was good at taping.

Ⓓ Charlie would have won the talent show.

Incorrect. Videotaping would have no effect on whether Charlie won the talent show.

TRY IT! How would this story have been different if it had taken place in a time before TV and video cameras had been invented? Write your ideas on the lines below.

_____

_____

_____

A

PRACTICE Identifying Setting

The **setting** of a story is where and when the story takes place. The setting of a story can affect what happens in the plot.

Read this story. As you read, look for clues that tell you where and when the events take place. Then answer the questions.

Evan had been sitting in the same seat for more than two hours, and he was grumpy, messy, and tired. But as tired as he was, Evan couldn't sleep. The noise of the engines kept him awake no matter how hard he tried to block out the sound. Evan looked out the window at the clouds. The sun was beginning to rise in the east. Evan felt as though he had lost a day. When he had left home, the sun had just set.

Evan looked at the tray on the foldout table. As he finished his breakfast he thought, "If I were home, I'd be sound asleep by now."

The crackle of a microphone filled the air. "We should be arriving in about ten minutes," a voice said. "Please check that your seatbelts are fastened, your tray tables are up, and your seats are in the upright position. If you look to your left, you will soon see the city."

1. Where does this story take place? What details helped you identify this?

_____

_____

2. During what time of day do the events take place? What details helped you know?

_____

_____

A

INSTRUCTION FOR VIDEO SURPRISE

STRATEGIES AND TIPS Identifying Cause and Effect

- A **cause** is the reason something happens. An **effect** is the result of what happens.

- One way to recognize cause and effect is to look for clue words such as *because, therefore, since,* and *as a result.* If clue words are not there to help you, you'll need to figure out cause-and-effect relationships from other clues. For example, when Charlie sees that the letter came from *Video Surprise* (cause), his eyes *nearly bug out of his head* (effect).

12 **In his last journal entry, Charlie is in a forgiving mood because**

Ⓕ he is planning a *Video Surprise* party.

Incorrect. Charlie is thinking about having a party, but this is not the cause of his forgiving mood.

Ⓖ he got his first letter by "snail mail" in a long time.

Incorrect. Getting the letter does not put Charlie in a forgiving mood.

Ⓗ the video wins a $500 prize.

Incorrect. Reread the last journal entry. The video is a finalist for the $500 prize, but it has not won yet.

Ⓙ the video is selected as a finalist for a $500 prize.

Correct. Because the video is selected as a finalist for the $500 prize (cause), Charlie is in a better mood (effect).

TRY IT! **Underline the cause and circle the effect in each item below. The first one is done for you.**

1. ("Song to Myself" was selected as a finalist) because it was so funny.

2. Woody taped Charlie without his brother's permission. As a result, Charlie was angry about being the subject of the video.

3. Charlie got home late because he had attended softball practice.

A

 **PRACTICE** Identifying Cause and Effect

A **cause** is the reason something happens. An **effect** is the result of what happens. As you read, think about how one event leads to another. One cause can have several effects. One effect can have several causes.

Read the following paragraph. Think about how one cause can have several effects. Then fill in the chart.

> The high temperatures of the past couple of weeks caused a lot of problems in Herman's town. Because of the heat, all of his neighbors and the stores in town were using air conditioners. This created an overload of electricity, which caused a blackout. Because of the lack of electricity during the blackout, everyone's refrigerator stopped working. A great deal of food was ruined. At night, all the houses were completely dark. When power was finally restored, Herman and his neighbors decided to conserve their use of electrical power so that another blackout would not occur.

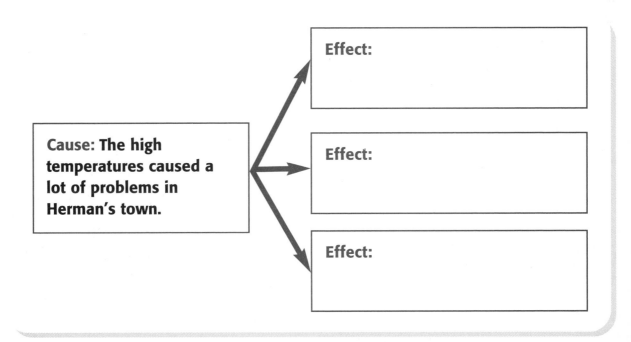

INSTRUCTION FOR VIDEO SURPRISE

STRATEGIES AND TIPS Drawing Conclusions

- When you **draw a conclusion,** you make a judgment or decision based on the details you have read in the story. When Charlie's mother tells him that he has mail, Charlie goes to check his computer. From this detail, you can draw the conclusion that Charlie thinks his mother meant that he has e-mail.

- After you have drawn a conclusion, go back to the story. Check the details to make sure that they support your conclusion.

13 **From the details in Charlie's journal, you can conclude that the TV show *Video Surprise* is**

Ⓐ a mystery show. | **Incorrect.** No details support the conclusion that *Video Surprise* is a mystery show.

Ⓑ a quiz show. | **Incorrect.** No details support the conclusion that *Video Surprise* is a quiz show.

Ⓒ a home video show. | **Correct.** Woody taped the video at home, and *Video Surprise* is a home video show.

Ⓓ a show that previews upcoming music videos. | **Incorrect.** Even though Charlie sings "Song to Myself," his video is not a real music video.

TRY IT! List two details from the story that support this conclusion: *Woody has a habit of getting on Charlie's nerves.*

1. _____

_____

2. _____

_____

 **PRACTICE** Drawing Conclusions

When you **draw a conclusion** about a character or event, you make a decision or judgment based on the details you have read.

Read the following letter about a school play.

Dear Derek,

Well, you missed the play of the century. The whole auditorium was packed. Elyse and Marco were great as the jewel thieves. They had the audience on the edge of their seats as they broke into the safe and then escaped.

Then, I entered as the detective. It wasn't exactly my finest moment. I tripped on a stool and went flying! Then half of my false moustache fell off my face. What a mess! The audience laughed hysterically. I tried to recover, but I forgot my lines! I tried to ad-lib, but all that came out was "Gadzooks! They've escaped!" Once again, the audience was rolling in the aisles.

Somehow the play was a big success, and I got a standing ovation! The drama club asked me to appear in their next play—*A Comedy of Errors*. I wonder why.

Your friend,
Ned

What conclusion can you draw about why the drama club wants Ned to be in their next play? Write two details that support your conclusion.

Conclusion: _____

Detail 1: _____

Detail 2: _____

A

Question 14 This question is about **identifying sequence** in a story.

STRATEGIES AND TIPS Identifying Sequence

- **Sequence** is the order in which events happen in a story. Sequence helps the reader understand what happens at the beginning, in the middle, and at the end of a story. As you read a story, look for *time* words, such as *before, after, then, next,* and *finally*. Look for words that tell you the time of day or the date. For example, the date of Charlie's first journal entry is Friday, April 10.

- Before you answer a question, read all the choices. Think back to the events you read about. In your mind, try to put the events in order.

14 **Which event happened *before* Charlie first got a letter from *Video Surprise*?**

F	Woody taped Charlie singing into a hairbrush.	**Correct.** Charlie tells that a few months ago Woody taped him singing into a hairbrush.
G	Charlie pleaded with his mother to tell the TV network not to run the tape.	**Incorrect.** This happened *after* Charlie received the first letter from *Video Surprise*.
H	Charlie decided that he might have a *Video Surprise* party.	**Incorrect.** Charlie gets the idea for a *Video Surprise* party after his mother refuses to call the TV network.
J	The video "Song to Myself" ran during the Teen Time segment of *Video Surprise*.	**Incorrect.** The letter from *Video Surprise* states that "Song to Myself" will air on May 26. In his journal, Charlie writes about receiving the letter on April 10.

TRY IT! **Number the events below in the order in which they happened.**

_____ "Song to Myself" is a finalist for the $500 prize.

_____ Charlie pleads with his mother to call the TV network and tell them not to run "Song to Myself."

_____ Woody tapes Charlie singing and dancing in front of a mirror.

PRACTICE Identifying Sequence

Sequence is the order in which events in a story happen. Sometimes an author will use words that signal time, such as *first, then, next,* and *finally.* Looking for the sequence, or order, will help you remember and understand what you read.

Read the following paragraph. As you read, look for time words that signal a sequence.

Raffi helps his father do the family laundry. First, they separate the whites from the colors. Then they get the soap and the bleach. Raffi's family uses the washing machines in the basement of their apartment house, so the next thing they do is take the elevator downstairs to the laundry room. After his dad puts the laundry and soap into the washing machines, Raffi puts four quarters into each machine. Finally, he turns on the machines, and he and his dad leave the laundry room.

Use the chart below to record the sequence of any three events in the paragraph.

A

Question 15 This question is about **analyzing characters** in a story.

STRATEGIES AND TIPS   Analyzing Character

- The characters of a story can be people, animals, or even imaginary beings, such as robots. An author helps a reader understand a **character** by describing the character through his or her actions, thoughts, or words.

- When you read a selection, look for words that tell how the character acts or what the character says, feels, or thinks. Pay attention to whether or not the character changes throughout the story. For example, at the beginning of this story, Charlie describes himself as being *furious, boiling, fuming,* and *irate.* But by the end, Charlie feels better about being on television.

15 **Which word *best* describes Charlie's feeling toward Woody by April 16?**

Ⓐ livid   **Incorrect.** This is how Charlie feels at the beginning of the story.

Ⓑ forgiving   **Correct. In his last journal entry, Charlie says that he is feeling forgiving.**

Ⓒ amused   **Incorrect.** Charlie's feelings have changed, but he doesn't think Woody is funny.

Ⓓ polite   **Incorrect.** There is nothing in the story that tells of Charlie being polite to Woody.

TRY IT!   **Write one word that describes Woody. Then tell why you chose that word.**

_____

_____

_____

A

PRACTICE **Analyzing Character**

You can try to understand a **character** in a story from the words used to describe what the character does, says, thinks, or feels.

Read the story below. Look for clues about Brad.

As Brad pulled open his closet door, a football, a pair of cleats, shoulder pads, and a football jersey came falling out. As he stared at the bulging closet, Brad shouted, "Mom, do you know what happened to my basketball uniform? Practice starts this week, and I have to have it!"

Mom called back, "I don't know where you put anything. I'm afraid even to go into your room, much less your closet. When did you last see your basketball uniform?"

"I don't know," shouted Brad.

Brad's mom rolled her eyes. "You're so forgetful, you'd lose your head if it weren't attached to your shoulders."

"She always says that," Brad muttered to himself. He kept searching. "I've got to clean up this mess," he thought.

"Brad," Mom called. "Manuel's on the phone."

"Hey, Manuel," Brad said on the phone. "What's up?"

"I found your basketball uniform in my gym bag."

"You did?" Brad asked. "How did it get there?"

Manuel laughed and said, "You know, buddy, you'd lose your head if . . . ."

"I know, I know," Brad interrupted.

Write one or two words that describe Brad. Then tell why you chose that word or words.

_____

_____

_____

A

STRATEGIES AND TIPS Identifying Details

- **Details** give the reader more information about a story. They help the reader organize information and keep events in order. Details give the **5Ws and H**: *who* the story is about, *what* the story is about, *where* and *when* it occurred, *why* an event occurred, and *how* it occurred.

- When you read for details, do not reread the entire selection. Skim the story to look for the information.

16 Which detail from Charlie's journal tells you that Woody sometimes reads it?

Ⓕ	Woody likes to use his parents' video camera.	**Incorrect.** This detail does not have anything to do with Charlie's journal.
Ⓖ	There is a message in the journal to Woody.	**Correct.** Charlie writes a message to Woody in case he reads Charlie's journal again.
Ⓗ	A letter arrives from *Video Surprise*.	**Incorrect.** There is nothing in the journal to indicate that Woody reads the journal entry about the letter.
Ⓙ	Charlie writes an invitation to a *Video Surprise* party.	**Incorrect.** This event is not mentioned anywhere in the journal.

TRY IT! Answer the following question with details from the story.

How did Charlie's mom try to persuade him that it wasn't necessary to ask the TV network not to show "Song to Myself"?

_____

_____

A

Details tell you more about people, places, things, and events. Details are the *who, what, when, where, why,* and *how* in stories you read.

Read the following story about Janet. Look for details that tell you *who, what, where, when, why,* and *how*.

It was 8:55 on a Friday night. Janet's dad was watching the end of a news special on TV. Janet and her mom were waiting for 9:00 so they could watch their favorite show.

"What was it like before TV?" Janet asked.

"Well," Mom replied, "I really don't know. We always had TV. But Grandma told me that she used to listen to the radio, play word games, read, and tell stories."

"Sounds boring," Janet said.

"Well, not according to Grandma," Mom answered.

"Time for your show," Dad said as he handed Mom the remote. Just then the TV went blank. "Uh, oh," Dad groaned. "Looks like the TV finally blew out."

"What are we going to do now?" Janet whined.

"We could look at these old pictures in our photo album," Mom suggested.

"Let's play checkers instead," Janet said, and Mom and Dad nodded in agreement.

Answer the following questions with details from the story.

1. Who is the story about? _____

2. What do they want to do but can't? _____

_____

3. How does Janet's family solve their problem? _____

_____

INSTRUCTION FOR VIDEO SURPRISE

A

TEST A
Selection 3

Directions: Read "Mia Hamm: Spotlight on Women's Sports" again. Then compare your answers with the answers given here.

Mia Hamm: Spotlight on Women's Sports

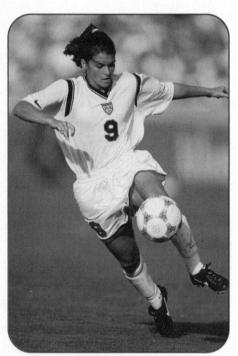

Mia Hamm plays in the 1996 Olympics.

consecutive: following one after another

poise: a state of calm or composure

On a dismal, rainy day, when many kids preferred to stay indoors, RFK Stadium in Washington, D.C. was packed with young female soccer fans. Hundreds of girls filled the stands, waiting to cheer for number 9, their soccer idol. Finally, their wait ended as Mia Hamm, the star player for the Washington Freedom, dashed onto the field.

Mia Hamm was actually much more than the star player for the Freedom. She was also the star player of the U.S. Women's National Team. Mia is probably the best all-around women's soccer player in the world.

In 1987, at the age of fifteen, Mia became the youngest player ever on the U.S. Women's National Soccer Team. Even four years later, in 1991, when the U.S. National Team won the World Championship, she was still the youngest player on the team. As a student at the University of North Carolina, she led her team to four **consecutive** national championships. Eventually, the school retired her number—19. No other University of North Carolina soccer player will wear that number.

It's not surprising to learn that Mia Hamm has had a significant impact on women's sports. Hamm's style of play, her **poise**, and her determination have set an example not only for soccer players but also for women competing in every sport. At the 1996 Atlanta Olympic Games,

© 2004 Options Publishing, Inc.

Mia led the U.S. team that won the gold medal. Eighty thousand fans witnessed the final match. This attendance set a record. Never before had so many people watched a women's sporting event.

Hamm has earned the praise of her fellow athletes for her quickness, speed, and will to succeed. Those who knew Mia as a young child, however, might not have predicted her success. Hamm credits growing up as one of six siblings with developing her competitive spirit. As Hamm herself recalls, she hated losing so much that she quit many of the various games she played with her siblings. She figured that if she quit before the game was over, she couldn't really lose. Then, when Mia was seven, she discovered soccer. Suddenly, the game wasn't just about winning and losing. Soccer was all about playing the game. From that point on, Mia's passion for the game has meant giving it her all for a win.

Hamm is also respected for more than her athletic ability. Though shy and soft-spoken and not one to seek out stardom, Hamm realizes that fame has given her an opportunity to promote women's sports. That's why you'll see her at girls' sports clinics and charity games all over the world.

Mia Hamm has also organized the Mia Hamm Foundation, which has two purposes. One is to help fight bone marrow disease, which killed her brother Garrett. The other is to develop further opportunities for young women who want to participate in sports.

Mia Hamm signs autographs after a game.

As the skies eventually brightened over RFK Stadium, the huge crowd of fans applauded. The team estimated that when Mia Hamm played, she'd bring an extra 3,000 to 5,000 people to the stadium. Many of the fans were girls like the ones who hang on the rails after the game, hoping for an autograph or a chance to talk with Mia. As Hamm moved along the fence, signing her name on their programs, these fans were not disappointed.

Go On ➡

Question 17 This question is about **identifying the author's purpose**.

STRATEGIES AND TIPS Identifying Author's Purpose

- The **author's purpose** is the reason an author has for writing. The purpose can be to *entertain, persuade, inform, explain,* or *describe* something or someone to the reader. In the article "Mia Hamm: Spotlight on Women's Sports," the author wants to inform you by giving facts about Mia Hamm and her soccer career.

- Knowing the author's purpose for writing can help you better understand what you are reading.

---

17 **What is the author's purpose for writing this article?**

Ⓐ to describe how to play soccer	**Incorrect.** The author does not describe how to play soccer.
Ⓑ to persuade the reader to play soccer	**Incorrect.** The author describes the soccer career of Mia Hamm. The author does not try to persuade the reader to play soccer.
Ⓒ to entertain the reader with humorous stories about soccer	**Incorrect.** The reader may find parts of the selection entertaining, but the selection was not written to entertain the reader.
Ⓓ to give readers information about Mia Hamm and her life	**Correct.** This is the author's main purpose. The author wants to give facts and information about the life of Mia Hamm.

TRY IT! The author's purpose is to inform you about Mia Hamm's life and soccer career. Skim the article. Write three things you learned about Mia from reading it.

1. _____

2. _____

3. _____

A

The most common purposes for writing are to *entertain, persuade, inform, explain,* or *describe*. If you know the **author's purpose** for writing, you can focus on what is important. An author may have more than one purpose for writing.

Read the article below.

Every year my family and I go to Lake Oscawana. We swim, fish, and go boating on the lake. The water used to be so pure that residents could use it for drinking water. This year, however, things were different. The water was murky, not crystal clear. Water plants choked the lake, and dead fish floated on the water. We realized that Oscawana was a dying lake.

At a town meeting we learned that the lake was being polluted. The cause was fertilizer from lawns that bordered the lake, and trash that people left behind. People decided that we had to take steps to save the lake.

What is the author's purpose for writing this article? Give your answer, along with two details that support your answer.

Purpose: _____

Detail: _____

_____

Detail: _____

_____

INSTRUCTION FOR MIA HAMM: SPOTLIGHT ON WOMEN'S SPORTS

A

STRATEGIES AND TIPS Identifying Cause and Effect

- A **cause** is the reason why something happens. An **effect** is the result of what happens. You will not always find clue words, such as *because* or *as a result,* to signal cause-and-effect relationships. Sometimes you have to infer, or figure out, the causes and effects.

- If you are not sure if two events are a cause and effect, link the two events with the words b*ecause, since,* or *as a result*. If the new sentence makes sense, then the two events are a cause-and-effect relationship.

18 Mia often quit the games she played with her siblings because

(F) she got tired of playing. **Incorrect.** This detail is not in the article.

(G) they were too competitive. **Incorrect.** There is nothing in the article that would suggest that her siblings were competitive.

(H) she hated losing. **Correct.** Mia thought that if she quit before the game was over, she couldn't really lose.

(J) the games did not involve quickness and speed. **Incorrect.** We do not know the kinds of games Mia played with her siblings.

TRY IT! Underline the cause and circle the effect in each of the following sentences. The first one is done for you.

1. Many young women go to watch Mia play because she is their idol.

2. Since Mia is such a good player, she has impacted women's sports.

3. Mia volunteers her time to worthy causes, so she is considered more than just an athlete.

A **cause** is the reason why something happens. An **effect** is the result of what happens. Often, one cause can have several effects.

Read the following news article. Think about how one cause can have several effects.

Sioux City

August 9

When Lulu Hudson saw the streak of light in the evening sky, she didn't know what to think. "It looked like a big comet," said Hudson. "It was scary." The streak of light was a meteorite heading for Hudson's cornfield. When it hit, the impact made a crater nine feet in diameter. The force of the blow knocked down the entire field of corn.

"I lost all that money for the corn," said Hudson, "but I opened a roadside attraction in its place. People from all over the country come to see that meteorite. So all's well that ends well."

Now complete the chart with the effects.

Cause: A meteorite hits Lulu Hudson's cornfield.

Effect:
Effect:
Effect:

STRATEGIES AND TIPS Classifying

- **Classifying** is grouping similar things together. When you read an article, you should be able to classify the ideas and details that go with the topic. For example, if the topic of an article is *sports,* you might look for details about soccer, basketball, and baseball. These can be classified, or grouped together, as sports.

- You may want to keep track of similar facts and details. For example, what do goalies, forwards, and sweepers all have in common? They can all be classified as players on a soccer team.

19 **Which answer *best* fits in Circle 1?**

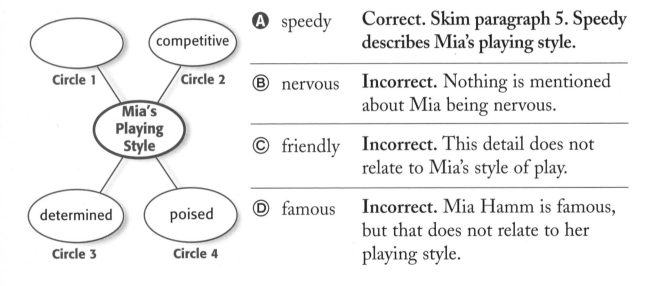

Ⓐ speedy   **Correct.** Skim paragraph 5. Speedy describes Mia's playing style.

Ⓑ nervous   **Incorrect.** Nothing is mentioned about Mia being nervous.

Ⓒ friendly   **Incorrect.** This detail does not relate to Mia's style of play.

Ⓓ famous   **Incorrect.** Mia Hamm is famous, but that does not relate to her playing style.

TRY IT! **For each list, cross out the item that does not belong. Then write a title that describes what the items have in common.**

1. necktie, water bottle, backpack, hiking boots

_____

2. violin, banjo, drum, guitar

_____

To **classify,** you group objects or ideas that are similar. You can better understand a topic if you can categorize ideas and information about that topic.

Read the paragraph. Think about the topic of the paragraph. Then look for details that can be grouped together under that topic.

There are many ways young people can volunteer in their towns or neighborhoods. By volunteering, you help someone in need. You also gain a sense of accomplishment. One way of helping is to run errands for an elderly person. You can walk a dog for a neighbor who is sick. You can read stories to a younger child. You might also offer to weed a garden for a neighbor. One group of kids cleaned out the areas around trees on their block. They planted flowers in them to beautify their neighborhood. That made everyone feel good!

Now fill in the chart.

Topic:
Detail:
Detail:
Detail:

INSTRUCTION FOR MIA HAMM: SPOTLIGHT ON WOMEN'S SPORTS

A

Question 20 This question is about **comparing and contrasting**.

STRATEGIES AND TIPS Comparing and Contrasting

- When you read an article, you may find it helpful to **compare** people, events, things, or ideas to see how they are alike. You might also want to **contrast** them, or see how they are different. "On a dismal, rainy day, when many kids preferred to stay indoors, RFK Stadium in Washington, D.C. was packed with young female soccer fans." Here, the author is contrasting young female soccer fans with many (other) kids.

- Clue words that tell you things are being compared are: *alike, same, both,* and *similarly.* Clue words that signal contrast include: *unlike, on the other hand,* and *different.*

---

20 Unlike the way Mia felt about games with her siblings, she now

F	feels passion for the game of soccer.	**Correct.** When Mia was young, playing games was about winning and losing. Now she plays soccer because she feels a passion for it.
G	always worries about losing in games.	**Incorrect.** She wants to win but doesn't worry about losing, as she did when she was younger.
H	often quits before the game is over.	**Incorrect.** This detail describes how she acted as a child.
J	doesn't really care if she wins or not.	**Incorrect.** Mia plays to win, though her focus is playing well.

TRY IT! Skim the article to find information on the Mia Hamm Foundation. Compare the two purposes of the foundation by telling how they are alike. Contrast them by telling how they are different.

1. **Compare:** _____

2. **Contrast:** _____

A

When authors **compare** people, events, things, or ideas, they describe how they are alike. When comparing, authors may use words such as *alike, same, both,* and *similarly*. When authors **contrast** people, events, things, or ideas, they describe how they are *different*. When contrasting, authors may use words such as *but, however, on the other hand,* and *different*.

Read each sentence or pair of sentences. Circle the word that signals that two things are alike or different. Then write the two things the author is comparing or contrasting. The first one is done for you.

1. I like the TV show *Roboman*. (However,) *Lewis and Son* makes me laugh more.

   Contrasting two TV shows
   _____

2. The beaches of Hawaii and the mountains of Alaska are both beautiful locations.

   _____

3. Thomas has dark, wavy hair. Unlike his twin, Richard has blond, curly hair.

   _____

4. Getting a new dog and getting a new cat are alike in many ways.

   _____

5. I like the movies. On the other hand, the rodeo is more exciting.

   _____

6. Both Carrie and I prefer oatmeal raisin cookies to peanut butter cookies.

   _____

© 2004 Options Publishing, Inc.

INSTRUCTION FOR MIA HAMM: SPOTLIGHT ON WOMEN'S SPORTS

A

STRATEGIES AND TIPS Identifying Fact and Opinion

- A **fact** is a statement that can be proved by checking in reference books, such as atlases and encyclopedias, or other sources. *Mia was the youngest woman ever to play for the U.S. National Soccer Team.* You could check this by looking in a record book, reading news articles, or checking Internet sites.

- An **opinion** is a statement that tells what someone feels or thinks. It cannot be proved or disproved. *The Mia Hamm Foundation is Mia's greatest contribution.* This is one person's opinion. Another person might disagree.

21 Which statement is an *opinion*?

Ⓐ No other University of North Carolina soccer player will wear that number. — **Incorrect.** This is a fact from the selection.

Ⓑ Hamm credits growing up as one of six siblings with developing her competitive spirit. — **Incorrect.** This is also a fact. You could ask Mia if it were true or false.

Ⓒ When Mia Hamm plays, she brings an extra 3,000 to 5,000 people to the stadium. — **Incorrect.** This is a fact that could be checked.

Ⓓ She is probably the best women's soccer player in the world. — **Correct.** This is an opinion. Some people might disagree.

TRY IT! Write *F* for fact or *O* for opinion before each statement below.

1. _____ Mia was number 9 on the Washington Freedom team.

2. _____ Covering women's soccer games is a challenging job.

3. _____ Women's soccer needs more players like Mia Hamm.

4. _____ Mia played soccer at the University of North Carolina.

© 2004 Options Publishing, Inc.

A

Remember, **facts** can be checked or proved, but **opinions** cannot.

Read this paragraph about Tyrone Simmons. Think about which sentences are facts and which are opinions.

Until recently, an empty lot on Mott Street was filled with trash and rubble. It was an eyesore that no one could make disappear. Mott Street resident Tyrone Simmons decided to do something about the problem. On weekends, he and other people from the neighborhood worked to clean up the trash and rubble. Once the lot was cleared, they planted trees, grass, shrubs, and flowers. Now the once empty lot is the most beautiful spot on Mott Street. Tyrone Simmons is certainly a Mott Street hero.

Fill in the chart with three facts and three opinions from the paragraph.

Facts	Opinions

Question 22 This question is about **identifying supporting details** in an article.

STRATEGIES AND TIPS) Identifying Supporting Details

- **Supporting details** support the main idea of an article, a section of an article, or a paragraph. Supporting details help make the main idea clear.

- For example, the author writes: "Hamm is also respected for more than her athletic ability." The author then gives supporting details that explain this idea: "Though shy and soft-spoken and not one to seek out stardom, Hamm realizes that fame has given her an opportunity to promote women's sports. That's why you'll see her at girls' sports clinics and charity games all over the world."

22 Which detail supports the idea that Mia Hamm has had a significant impact on women's sports?

Ⓕ Those who knew Mia as a young child, however, might not have predicted her success.	**Incorrect.** This is true, but the way Mia was when she was a child does not support the idea that she has had a significant impact on women's sports.
Ⓖ Hamm is also respected for more than her athletic ability.	**Incorrect.** This is true, but it is not important to her impact on women's sports.
Ⓗ Soccer was all about playing the game.	**Incorrect.** This supports the idea that Mia loves soccer.
Ⓙ Never had so many people watched a women's sports event.	**Correct.** Mia's ability to get people to watch her play impacts women's sports.

TRY IT! Find two details that support this idea: *She has also organized the Mia Hamm Foundation, which has two purposes.*

1. _____

2. _____

A

 **PRACTICE** | Identifying Supporting Details

Supporting details support or build on the main idea. Without supporting details, the main idea may be hard to understand.

Read the following paragraph. Look for three details that support the idea that Roy Chapman Andrews made important discoveries. Write them on the lines.

In the early 1920s, Roy Chapman Andrews and a team of scientists set out for the Gobi Desert of Mongolia. Andrews believed that many fossils of dinosaurs and ancient mammals could be found there. Indeed, Andrews and his team made many important discoveries. Within days, they found the fossil bones of an extinct rhinoceros. Later, they uncovered a nest of the first dinosaur eggs ever seen. Up to that time, scientists were not sure if dinosaurs gave birth to live young or if they laid eggs. Perhaps Andrews's most important find in those years was a very small mammal fossil. Before then, the few mammal fossils from the Age of Dinosaurs belonged to mammal groups that had died out. This one, however, was related to those alive today. Over the years, Andrews collected hundreds of dinosaur and extinct mammal fossils. Many of them are on display at the American Museum of Natural History in New York.

Supporting Details

1. _____

2. _____

3. _____

STRATEGIES AND TIPS Making Inferences

- When you **make inferences,** you make logical guesses. You use the information in the article, along with your own common sense.

- When an event happens in an article, think about why it happens and what it might mean. Use the information and what you know to make an inference. From the information in the article about Mia Hamm and what you already know, you can tell that she is a good sport when she plays.

23 **From the article, you can infer, or guess, that Mia Hamm**

(A) hates playing games with her siblings.

Incorrect. She hated losing, not playing.

(B) likes to be on TV.

Incorrect. She plays soccer on TV, but there is nothing in the article that tells how she feels about it. It is not anything that a reader would have to infer.

(C) gets tired of meeting her fans.

Incorrect. She seems to like her fans, but it isn't clear that she tires of it.

(D) is generous with her time and money.

Correct. Using the details and your common sense you could infer that Hamm is generous with her time and money.

TRY IT! List two details from the article that support this inference: *Mia Hamm was a successful soccer player when she played at the University of North Carolina.*

1. _____

_____

2. _____

_____

In an article, you may need to find clues and then make your own **inferences,** or logical guesses, about the topic. Use these clues and your own knowledge and common sense to infer.

Read the following news article about a baseball team.

Howard High Falls to White Plains

The Howard High School baseball team leads the league in batting and home runs scored. But Saturday turned ugly as Howard High lost to White Plains High by a score of 13–2. Disaster struck early, when pitcher Darryl Williams left the game with a stomachache. In the second inning, White Plains player John Chen hit a homer with the bases loaded. In the fourth inning, two more players from Howard left the game with stomachaches.

"None of my players were feeling well," said Coach Dan Hardy. "My goal was just to get through the game. I canceled practice tomorrow. Hopefully my players can rest and get better for next week's game."

What inference can you make about the players on the Howard High team? Write on the lines below. Fill in two details that helped you.

Inference: _____

_____

Detail 1: _____

_____

Detail 2: _____

_____

INSTRUCTION FOR MIA HAMM: SPOTLIGHT ON WOMEN'S SPORTS

A

STRATEGIES AND TIPS Identifying Sequence

- **Sequence** is the order in which events are presented in a selection. The events may not always be written in the order in which they happened in time. In "Mia Hamm: Spotlight on Women's Sports," for example, the author begins the article with an event that happened recently. Then the author goes back to events in Mia's past.

- As you read a selection, look for time words such as *before, after, then, next,* and *finally.*

24 **Which of the following events happened *first* in Mia's life?**

F	Mia played for the Washington Freedom.	**Incorrect.** Mia played on this team later in her career.
G	Mia played soccer at the 1991 World Championships.	**Incorrect.** Read paragraph 3 carefully. This event happened after she played for the U.S. National Team.
H	Mia became a member of the U.S. National Soccer Team.	**Correct.** This is the first of the four events listed. She played on the National Team before the World Championships.
J	Mia played soccer at the University of North Carolina.	**Incorrect.** She played at the university after playing on the World Championship team.

TRY IT! **Choose three events from Mia Hamm's life. Using the words *first, then,* and *finally,* write three sentences that tell the order in which the events occurred.**

1. _____

2. _____

3. _____

As you read, look for the **sequence,** or order, that will help you remember and understand what you read.

Read this paragraph from a nature magazine. Look for words such as *before, after, then, next,* and *finally* that signal a sequence. Remember, not every event will have a signal word.

There are four stages in a butterfly's life, which includes metamorphosis. First, a butterfly lays an egg on or near a plant. After a few weeks, the egg hatches and a caterpillar appears. The hungry caterpillar spends most of its time eating. Then it makes a hard protective case around itself. This is the pupa stage. Within the case, the caterpillar is transformed into a butterfly. Finally, the butterfly emerges and flies away.

Circle the time signal words in the paragraph. Then use the chart below to record the sequence of four events in the paragraph. Write what happens after a butterfly lays an egg.

INSTRUCTION FOR MIA HAMM: SPOTLIGHT ON WOMEN'S SPORTS

A

© 2004 Options Publishing, Inc.

Directions: Read "Medio-Pollito's Bad Luck" again. Then compare your answers with the answers given here.

Medio-Pollito's Bad Luck

tortilla (tor-TEE-yuh): a round, flat bread rolled out into the shape of a pancake

adios (ah-dee-OHSS): the Spanish word meaning "goodbye"

Long ago, a fine black hen waited for her brood to hatch. The first several chicks to hatch were plump, but the last one was a sight to behold! He was as flat as a **tortilla**, with one eye, one leg, one ear, and one pitiful wing. His mother named him Medio-Pollito (MAY-dee-oh poh-YEE-toh), which in Spanish means "half-chick."

The other chicks were well-behaved and stuck close to the farmyard, pecking for grubs in the dirt. But Medio-Pollito was not content to stay by his mother's side. He wanted to travel to see the king. One day, without so much as an **adios** to his dear Mama, Medio-Pollito hopped down the dusty road.

Soon he came to a river. "Medio-Pollito," called Water, "please come and help me. A log has fallen across my middle, and I am rising over my banks."

"I'm too busy to stop," laughed Medio-Pollito. "I'm on my way to see the king!"

The chick hopped along the road. Soon he passed a campfire smoldering on the ground.

"Medio-Pollito," called out Fire, "please feed me some sticks quickly or I shall go out!"

But Medio-Pollito hopped on without a pause. "I have more important things to do," he called over his narrow shoulder.

Not long after, Medio-Pollito passed a tall tree with a large wind caught in its branches. "Please, Medio-Pollito," implored Wind, "I am all tangled up, and I must continue to blow north. Won't you help me?" The half-chick hopped on his way, too hurried to lend a hand.

Soon he arrived at the palace gate. "Half a chicken!" exclaimed a man, grabbing the chick. It was the chef, preparing soup for the king's dinner. He plopped the chick right into a soup pot filled with water.

"Water," begged Medio-Pollito, "please save me!"

"I once asked you for help," Water responded. "I cannot help you now."

The chef carried the pot to the fire. "Please, Fire, help me!" squawked the half-chick.

Fire answered hotly, "You were in such a hurry before that you would not stop for me. Now **fend** for yourself."

fend: get along without help

Medio-Pollito hopped up and down in the boiling broth. He managed to escape from the soup, only to scorch his wing on the flames. Since the chick was no longer good for soup, the chef picked up the bird with the blackened wing and tossed him out the window.

Medio-Pollito hopped away, thinking that he was free. Just then, however, Wind blew by, scooped up Medio-Pollito, and dropped him on the highest rooftop. There he remains to this very day—a weather vane—pointing out which direction Wind blows.

Go On ➡

A

> ## STRATEGIES AND TIPS Identifying Sequence
>
> - **Sequence** is the order in which events in a story happen. Sequence helps you understand what happens at the beginning, in the middle, and at the end of a story. As you read a story, look for time words, such as *before, after, then, next,* and *finally*. For example, "Not long after, Medio-Pollito passed a tall tree." The words *not long after* tell you when that event occurred.
>
> - Before you answer a question, think back to the story and put the events in order.

25 **Which event happened just *after* Medio-Pollito left home?**

Ⓐ Medio-Pollito came to a fire smoldering on the ground.

Incorrect. This was not the first thing that happened after Medio-Pollito left home.

Ⓑ The chef at the palace plopped Medio-Pollito into a soup pot.

Incorrect. This event happened toward the end of the story.

Ⓒ Medio-Pollito came to a tree with the wind caught in its branches.

Incorrect. Medio-Pollito had been traveling for some time when this event occurred.

Ⓓ Medio-Pollito came to a river that was going to flood its banks.

Correct. This event occurred just after Medio-Pollito left home.

TRY IT! On his journey, Medio-Pollito met Water, Fire, and Wind. Using the words *first, next,* and *finally*, write three sentences that tell the order in which he met each of them.

1. _____

2. _____

3. _____

PRACTICE Identifying Sequence

An author often presents the events of a story in the order in which they occur. As you read a story, look for the **sequence,** or order of events.

Read the following story. Look for time words that signal a sequence.

Fox wanted to bake a cake for Rabbit's birthday. First, Fox got all the things he needed. Next, he mixed the batter for the cake. Then, he put the cake in the oven to bake. While the cake was baking, Fox made the frosting. After the cake cooled, Fox frosted it.

That evening, Fox surprised his friend Rabbit with the cake. "A carrot cake!" said Rabbit. "It's my favorite!"

Circle the time words in the story. Then use the chart below to record the sequence in the story. The first one is done for you.

First, Fox gets all the things he needs.
↓
↓
↓
↓

Question 26 This question is about **identifying details** in a story.

STRATEGIES AND TIPS Identifying Details

- **Details** give you the basic **5Ws and H** in a story: *who, what, when, where, why,* and *how*. Paying attention to details in a story can help you organize the information and keep events in order.

- When you are asked to recall a detail, do not reread the entire selection. Think about where in the story you are most likely to find the detail. Then skim that section to look for the information.

26 Which detail tells you how Medio-Pollito got his name?

Ⓕ Medio-Pollito hopped up and down in the boiling broth.	**Incorrect.** This detail tells what happened when Medio-Pollito was dropped in the soup pot.
Ⓖ Wind dropped Medio-Pollito on the highest rooftop.	**Incorrect.** This detail tells how Medio-Pollito became a weather vane.
Ⓗ Medio-Pollito was as flat as a tortilla, with one eye, one leg, one ear, and one pitiful wing.	**Correct.** This answer is in the first paragraph.
Ⓙ Medio-Pollito was not content to stay by his mother's side.	**Incorrect.** This detail does not tell how Medio-Pollito got his name.

TRY IT! Look for details in the story to help you answer the following questions. Write the details on the lines.

1. Why did Medio-Pollito leave home?

_____

2. How did Medio-Pollito become a weather vane?

_____

A

PRACTICE Identifying Details

Details tell you more information about people, places, things, and events. Details tell the *who, what, when, where, why,* and *how* of what you read.

Read the following story about Casey. Look for details that tell you *who, what, when, where, why,* and *how*.

It was 9:00 on a Monday night. Casey sat at the desk in his bedroom. He was busy finishing a book report that was due the next day. He carefully typed the last sentence and then clicked the print icon. The printer began to hum. Then the computer screen went blank.

"No!" shouted Casey. "Mom, Dad! Help! Something is wrong with my computer."

Dad sat down at the computer. After a few minutes he shook his head. "You have a computer virus," he said. "It looks as though the virus ate your homework. Did you save the file?"

"No," said Casey, "But I have my notes. I'll write the book report by hand."

Use the chart below to record some of the details.

Who	
What	
Where	
How	

Question 27 This question is about **understanding plot** in a story.

STRATEGIES AND TIPS   Understanding Plot

- **Plot** is what happens in a story. The important events in the story make up the plot.

- The plot often involves a problem or conflict that a main character must somehow resolve. How a main character solves his or her problem is an important part of a story's plot.

- Recalling and understanding important events in a story can help you identify and understand other story elements, such as character, setting, and theme.

27 **What unexpected event occurs when Medio-Pollito arrives at the palace?**

Ⓐ He becomes a weather vane.   **Incorrect.** This event happens long after Medio-Pollito arrives at the palace.

Ⓑ He argues with the chef.   **Incorrect.** The story does not tell the time Medio-Pollito argues with the chef.

Ⓒ He does not stop to help the fire.   **Incorrect.** Medio-Pollito's refusal to stop to help the fire happens before he reaches the palace.

Ⓓ The chef grabs him and drops him into the soup.   **Correct.** Medio-Pollito was expecting to see the king, not become his dinner.

TRY IT!   After Medio-Pollito is thrown out of the window, he hops away, thinking that he is free. What unexpected event happens that changes the story's ending?

_____

_____

_____

PRACTICE) **Understanding Plot**

Plot is what happens in a story. The plot may involve a problem that the main character has to resolve.

Read the following story. Think about Fox's problem.

> Fox was walking through an orchard one sunny fall day when he spied a most delicious-looking apple. "I must have that apple," he said to himself, "but I cannot climb all the way out on that limb to get it. What shall I do?"
>
> Just then, Rabbit hopped by. "Do you see that apple?" said Fox. "I must have it. But I cannot reach it. You're known for being clever, Rabbit. Do you have an idea?"
>
> "That's simple," said Rabbit. "Just get the farmer's ladder and lean it against the tree."
>
> "No," said Fox, "I cannot climb out on that limb."
>
> "Suit yourself," said Rabbit, and he hopped away.
>
> The more Fox looked at the apple, the more he wanted it. He longed for it so, that he began to weep. Squirrel came to see what the noise was all about.
>
> "It's that apple," Fox said between sniffs. "I must have it and I cannot reach it."
>
> "Is that all?" said Squirrel. "Anything to quiet a loud, annoying fox." With that, she bit through the stem of the apple and down it tumbled, right at Fox's feet.
>
> "Why, thank you, my dear Squirrel," said Fox. And to himself he said, "Why didn't I think of crying sooner?"

On the lines below, describe Fox's problem and how he solves it.

_____

_____

_____

A

Question 28 This question is about **understanding theme** in a story.

STRATEGIES AND TIPS Understanding Theme

- The **theme** is the message of a story. The theme sometimes relates to a lesson the main character learns—or does not learn.

- Be careful not to confuse the theme of a story with its topic. The topic refers to what the story is about. The theme is the message or lesson to be learned from what happens in the story.

- When identifying the theme of a story, think about important events. What was the main character like at the beginning of the story? What was the character like at the end of the story? What happened to change him or her? What lesson did he or she learn?

28 **What is the theme of this story?**

ⓕ Goodness overcomes evil.

Incorrect. The events of this story do not address good and evil.

ⓖ If you are determined and work hard, you will succeed.

Incorrect. Medio-Pollito was determined but did not work hard. He did not succeed at his goal.

ⓗ If you do not help others, they may not help you when you need them.

Correct. Medio-Pollito did not help others. When he needed help, they would not help him.

ⓙ Prepare before starting a long journey.

Incorrect. Preparing for a journey was not dealt with in the story.

TRY IT! **Find three details in the story that support the theme: *If you do not help others, they may not help you.***

1. _____

2. _____

3. _____

A

The **theme** is the message or lesson of a story. A theme can be about ways characters deal with events in their lives.

Read the following story. Think about its theme.

More than anything else, Pilar wanted to be on the soccer team. Pilar loved soccer and she was a good player, but she wasn't sure that she was good enough to make the team. Tryouts were three weeks away. Each day after school she practiced. One day she practiced moving the ball up and down the field. Another day she practiced kicking goals. Her brother, Felipe, often practiced with her. Together they would race up and down the field, passing the ball.

On the day of the tryouts, Pilar tried her best. "How did it go?" asked Felipe when she returned home.

"I did great, but I don't know if I made the team," she said. "I'll have to wait."

A few days later, the coach posted the team roster. Pilar's hard work had paid off. Her name was at the top of the list.

Write the theme of the story below. Then, write two details from the story that support the theme.

Theme: _____

Detail 1: _____

_____

Detail 2: _____

_____

A

INSTRUCTION FOR MEDIO-POLLITO'S BAD LUCK

STRATEGIES AND TIPS Identifying Genre

- **Genre** is the type of literature you read. **Fiction** includes stories with characters and events that are made up. Myths, folktales, fables, short stories, and realistic fiction are fiction.

- As you read fiction, think about what kind of story it is. "Medio-Pollito's Bad Luck" is a *folktale,* a story that is passed on from generation to generation. Folktales may include animals that talk, or they may tell a story about how something came to be. Many folktales teach a lesson.

29 How can you tell that "Medio-Pollito's Bad Luck" is a folktale?

Ⓐ It is about real events that happen to real people. | **Incorrect.** There are no real people in the story. The story is made up.

Ⓑ It is a story that has talking animals and teaches a lesson. | **Correct. The story has animal characters and it teaches a lesson.**

Ⓒ It takes place in the future. | **Incorrect.** The story does not take place in the future.

Ⓓ It is about chickens. | **Incorrect.** The story is about chickens, but this does not make it a folktale.

TRY IT! On the lines below, write two reasons why this story cannot be called realistic fiction.

1. _____

_____

2. _____

_____

A

Fiction includes stories that are made up. *Folktales* are stories that teach a lesson or explain how something came to be.

Read the following passage from a story. As you read, look for clues to help you identify the kind of fiction it is.

Long ago, in a faraway land, there lived a tailor. The tailor was a hard-working man. Each day he cut cloth and sewed, making fancy suits and coats for noblemen. Even though he worked long hours, he barely made enough money to put food on the table for his poor family. One day a nobleman came to his shop. "I want you to make me a coat. I'll need it tomorrow," snapped the nobleman.

The tailor cut the cloth and began sewing. He knew it would be impossible to finish the coat by the next day. Still, he tried. Past midnight, he fell asleep at his table. While he slept, three elves appeared. They quickly got to work. One elf sewed the sleeves. Another elf sewed on the buttons. The third elf attached the beautiful gold trim. When the tailor awoke the next morning, the shimmering coat hung before him.

1. Circle the kind of fiction this story reflects.

realistic fiction   folktale

2. Tell how you know.

_____

_____

(STRATEGIES AND TIPS) **Analyzing Character**

- The **characters** of a story can be people, animals, or even imaginary beings, such as robots. An author helps a reader understand a character by describing the character through his or her actions, thoughts, or words.

- When you read, look for words that tell how the character feels, what the character does, and how the character thinks.

30 **Which word *best* describes Medio-Pollito's feelings toward Fire, Water, and Wind?**

Ⓕ courageous — **Incorrect.** The details do not support the idea that Medio-Pollito had courage.

Ⓖ helpful — **Incorrect.** Throughout the story, Medio-Pollito refused to help anyone.

Ⓗ uncaring — **Correct.** This best describes Medio-Pollito. He did not care that others needed help.

Ⓙ concerned — **Incorrect.** This is the opposite of Medio-Pollito's attitude. He was not concerned at all about others.

TRY IT! **Read the sentences below. What do they tell you about what Medio-Pollito is like? Write your answer on the lines.**

"He wanted to travel to see the king. One day, without so much as an *adios* to his dear Mama, Medio-Pollito hopped down the dusty road."

_____

_____

_____

_____

© 2004 Options Publishing, Inc.

One way to understand a **character** is to look for details that tell you about the character's actions, thoughts, or words.

Read the following paragraph about May. As you read, look for words that describe May's actions, thoughts, and feelings.

The pouring rain began to seep down the back of May's raincoat. She pulled the collar tightly around her neck and bent her head against the wind as she made her way home through the storm. It was then that she saw the dripping-wet puppy huddled against a tree. "The poor little thing," she thought. The tiny animal wagged its tail when it saw her. May scooped up the wet bundle and covered it with her raincoat. "You're coming home with me," she said softly.

Complete the sentence to describe what May is like. Then write three details from the paragraph that support your answer.

May is _____

1. _____

_____

2. _____

_____

3. _____

_____

A

STRATEGIES AND TIPS Drawing Conclusions

- When you **draw a conclusion,** you make a decision based on the information in the story. After Medio-Pollito burns his wing in the fire, the chef tosses him out the window. From this detail, you can draw the conclusion that the chef knew a burnt chick would not make a good soup.

- After you have drawn a conclusion, go back to the story. Check the details to make sure they support your conclusion.

31 **From the details in the story, what conclusion can you draw about Wind?**

Ⓐ Wind blows Medio-Pollito up to the rooftop to punish him.

Correct. You can conclude that Wind was punishing Medio-Pollito because he had not helped Wind earlier in the story.

Ⓑ Wind likes Medio-Pollito and wants to help him.

Incorrect. No details support the conclusion that Wind likes Medio-Pollito.

Ⓒ Wind blows out the fire under the soup pot to save Medio-Pollito.

Incorrect. This is not a detail from the story.

Ⓓ Wind wants to teach Medio-Pollito how to fly.

Incorrect. Wind blew Medio-Pollito to the rooftop to punish him, not to teach him how to fly.

TRY IT! List two details from the story that support this conclusion: *Medio-Pollito was in a hurry to see the king.*

1. _____

_____

2. _____

_____

When you **draw a conclusion,** you make a logical guess or decision based on the details you have read.

Read the following letter that Marty wrote to his grandmother.

Dear Grandma,

The science fair was a lot of fun but not what I expected. My model of the volcano looked very real. All the kids in my class loved it. I had planned to set off the eruption and lava flow when the judge got to my booth. But things didn't go exactly as planned. The eruption was a little more forceful than I had thought it would be. It blew the top off the volcano. The judge wound up with lava all over his suit. He was not happy!

Well, I was definitely disappointed when the awards were given out, but I am not discouraged. I am going to start building a new volcano tomorrow. I'll have it ready when you come for a visit. This time it will work.

Love,
Marty

What conclusion can you draw about whether or not Marty won a prize at the science fair? Write your conclusion. Then list details from the letter that support your conclusion.

Conclusion: _____

Detail 1: _____

Detail 2: _____

Detail 3: _____

INSTRUCTION FOR MEDIO-POLLITO'S BAD LUCK

STRATEGIES AND TIPS   Using Context Clues

- **Context clues** are the words, phrases, and sentences surrounding an unfamiliar word. These clues can help you figure out the meaning of the unfamiliar word. Sometimes, an unfamiliar word is defined. For example: "Not long after, Medio-Pollito passed a tall tree with a large wind caught in its branches. 'Please, Medio-Pollito,' implored Wind, 'I am all <u>tangled</u> up.'" The phrase *caught in its branches* helps you know what *tangled* means.

- Replace the unfamiliar word in the test sentence with each answer choice. Decide which word makes the most sense.

32 "He managed to escape from the soup, only to *scorch* his wing on the flames." What does the word *scorch* mean?

Ⓕ	to dry	**Incorrect.** Replace *scorch* with *dry*. It does not make sense.
Ⓖ	to warm	**Incorrect.** If his wing were only warm, the chef would have left him in the soup.
Ⓗ	to burn	**Correct.** Medio-Pollito's wing went on the flames, and then it became blackened. Flames can burn and turn things black. *Scorch* means "to burn."
Ⓙ	to get wet	**Incorrect.** One does not get wet falling into a fire.

TRY IT! Read these sentences. Circle words or phrases that help you understand the meaning of each underlined word.

1. Medio-Pollito is <u>disobedient</u>. He does not obey his mother and runs away from home.

2. The chicken treats Water, Wind, and Fire with great <u>disdain</u>. He does not care about their problems and barely speaks to them as he rushes on.

PRACTICE Using Context Clues

Context clues are hints to the meaning of an unfamiliar word. These hints may be words or phrases in the sentences around the unfamiliar word.

Read the following groups of sentences. Use context clues to help you understand the meaning of the underlined word. Then write a definition of the word.

1. The old dog Truman lay in the barnyard. He was <u>perplexed</u> by Tammy the Cat's behavior. He simply could not understand why Tammy wanted to leave the comfort of their farm for the noise and bustle of the city.

_____

2. With hammers, the scientists chipped away at the ancient <u>shale</u>. Suddenly, they stared in wonder at the hundreds of fossils contained in the layered rock.

_____

3. Last year, the crops had <u>flourished</u>. This year, the story was different. Almost nothing grew. Everywhere, dead or dying plants dropped in the fields.

_____

4. From the beginning, the play was a <u>fiasco</u>. The curtain would not go up. The actors forgot their lines. The lights would not dim. "It's a disaster!" sobbed Elaine, the playwright.

_____

5. The knight had <u>blatantly</u> stolen the king's golden cup right in front of everyone. He had made no effort to hide his actions.

_____

A

TEST B

Selection 1   Directions: **Read this article about alligators. Then answer Questions 1–8.**

Gators!

> **wetland:** marshy land; land where there is much moisture in the soil. Wetlands are important to the survival of many animals and plants and to the food chain of which they are part.

Scientists have learned a lot about the American alligator. They know that alligators are an important part of the **wetland** environment in the southeastern United States. To save alligators, scientists study them to learn more about how and where they live.

Alligators are reptiles, which means that they are cold-blooded animals. The body temperature of a cold-blooded animal depends on the temperature of the surrounding air. If an alligator is too cold, it cannot move very quickly. It must search for a warmer place. If it is too warm, it will move to a cooler place to lower its body temperature. By using the air temperature around them, alligators are able to control their body temperature.

Alligators, or gators, are nocturnal. They are active at night. They are also carnivorous. Gators love to eat meat. They eat turtles, snakes, and other small animals. When gators float at the water's edge, they look like brown logs. Only their eyes and nostrils, or noses, show above the water.

When an animal comes to the water's edge to drink, the gator

Adult alligators are on the average 6 to 8 feet long.

© 2004 Options Publishing, Inc.

swings its powerful tail, knocking the prey into the water. The gator's sharp teeth lock around the prey and drag it under the water. The gator drowns larger victims before it tears them into pieces and swallows them.

Gators use their claws and long snouts to dig burrows at the edge of the water.

An alligator hatchling

These burrows are called "gator holes." Gators use these holes to store uneaten food, hide from danger, and hibernate during cold weather.

Female alligators make a mound of mud and sticks that they use as a nest in wetland areas. They lay between forty and seventy hard-shelled eggs in the nest. The hatchlings, or baby alligators, are about six inches long. Raccoons, otters, birds, and snakes eat most of them. Only a few hatchlings survive to become adults.

Adult gators have few enemies, except for humans. At one time, hunters killed them for their meat and hide, or skin. Alligator hide was used to make leather for shoes, wallets, and other items. These items were very popular for a while.

Because of hunting, alligators were in danger of becoming **extinct**. In 1967, the United States government added alligators to the endangered species list. Laws were passed to stop people from hunting gators. This saved the American alligator. Today, they are no longer endangered. However, people must continue to protect alligators. They are important to the survival of the wetland environment.

extinct: no longer existing

Go On ➡

© 2004 Options Publishing, Inc.

1 **This article is *mostly* about**

Ⓐ how alligators raise their young.

Ⓑ why alligators were endangered.

Ⓒ how alligators live in their environment.

Ⓓ the effects of being a cold-blooded animal.

2 **Which detail *best* supports the main idea of the article?**

Ⓕ Gators use their claws and long snouts to dig burrows at the edge of the water.

Ⓖ Alligator hide was used to make shoes and wallets.

Ⓗ In 1967, the United States government added alligators to the endangered species list.

Ⓙ The hatchlings are about six inches long.

3 **Which detail supports the conclusion that laws have helped alligators survive?**

Ⓐ People must continue to protect alligators.

Ⓑ Only a few hatchlings survive to become adults.

Ⓒ Today, alligators are no longer endangered.

Ⓓ Raccoons, otters, birds, and snakes eat most of the baby alligators.

4 **What does a female alligator do *after* she makes a mound of mud and sticks?**

Ⓕ She knocks her prey into the water.

Ⓖ She moves to a cooler place to lower her body temperature.

Ⓗ She lays between forty and seventy eggs in the nest.

Ⓙ She waits and listens for the baby alligators to hatch.

5 Which answer *best* fits in Circle 1?

Ⓐ wetlands

Ⓑ endangered

Ⓒ raccoons

Ⓓ carnivorous

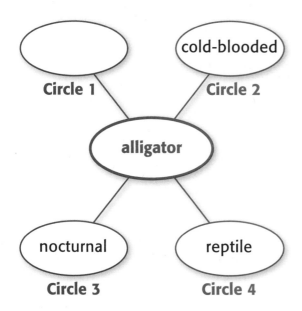

6 Because alligators are cold-blooded, they

Ⓕ have poor eyesight.

Ⓖ tear their prey to pieces before swallowing them.

Ⓗ float at the water's edge.

Ⓙ use the air temperature to control their body temperature.

7 Which of the following statements is an *opinion*?

Ⓐ Alligators are the scariest animals in the water.

Ⓑ Only a few alligator hatchlings survive to become adults.

Ⓒ Some people killed alligators for their meat.

Ⓓ Scientists have learned a lot about the American alligator.

8 "Alligators, or gators, are *nocturnal*. They are active at night." The word *nocturnal* means

Ⓕ active during the day.

Ⓖ active during the night.

Ⓗ plant eaters.

Ⓙ meat eaters.

Directions: **Read this story about an unusual form of entertainment. Then answer Questions 9–16.**

Something New

Friday after basketball practice, Veronica and I shared a bowl of popcorn at her house. When we had finished, I noticed a funny design "dancing" across the bottom of the bowl. Knowing Veronica as well as I do, I recognized her signature doodle—a pattern of swirls, stars, and basketballs. I asked her where she had gotten the bowl.

Veronica explained that she'd painted the bowl herself at a place called The Clay Room. She asked me if I wanted to try it. I have to admit, I didn't really want to go. Painting bowls sounded pretty boring to me. But after a while, she talked me into it.

The next day, Veronica and I set off for The Clay Room. When we arrived, we stood admiring the colorful pieces displayed in the window. One mug was adorned with a beautiful green and blue **mosaic** decoration.

> mosaic: a design with small colored squares

Inside, Veronica introduced me to Amy, who runs the shop. I explained that I had never painted pottery before because it had never interested me. "Well, Ben," replied Amy, "the best way to change your mind is to try it." Amy explained that the first step was to choose the pieces we wanted to make. I decided on a mug. Veronica chose a coin bank.

"The next step," Amy explained, "is to choose an image or design you'd like to paint on your piece." She ushered us to a table scattered

with stencils, or patterns, and books with design ideas. Here we chose our designs.

"Next, you choose the background color," said Amy. She showed us a group of bottles filled with pottery paints, or glazes. She explained that before the pieces are heated, or fired, the paints appear pale and chalky. As they are heated, the colors change and darken. You really have to use your imagination to picture the look of the finished piece.

Amy picked up a dish painted a wispy yellow to show the see-through look that results from one coat of paint. She then picked up a bright blue box. "For this look, you need to use three coats of paint," she said.

She rotated the box slightly to show a hardened bubble **marring** the surface. Amy explained, "This is what happens if you don't let the paint dry after each coat. Moisture becomes trapped between the layers." She explained that when such a piece is fired at 2,000 degrees in the **kiln**, the moisture boils and bubbles.

> **marring:** damaging or spoiling

> **kiln:** an oven used to bake or harden clay

After applying the base coat, it's time to paint the design. "Again," she said, "you have to be careful of the colors you use." She held up a plate on which a green moon floated on a background of midnight blue. It had an eerie effect. Amy explained that the moon had originally been bright yellow. "The painter forgot that glazes change color in the kiln," she explained. "When the plate was heated, the dark blue showed through the yellow, turning the moon green."

Veronica and I spent the afternoon working on our pieces. I sure found out one thing: Getting pottery painting right is quite a challenge! But it's lots of fun. All I have to do is to look at my new green mug with its bright yellow star to remember this.

Go On ➡

9 Hardened bubbles mar the surface of a pot as a result of

 Ⓐ painting the design incorrectly.

 Ⓑ forgetting that glazes change colors in the kiln.

 Ⓒ being careless with the colors you use.

 Ⓓ not waiting for the paint to dry after each coat.

10 How was Ben's mug different from the mug he saw in the window?

 Ⓕ His mug had a bubbled glaze, but the one in the window didn't.

 Ⓖ The mug in the window sparkled, but his had a dull look.

 Ⓗ The mug in the window had a blue and green mosaic pattern, but his was green with a yellow star.

 Ⓙ His mug was easy to make, whereas the one in the window had been difficult to make.

11 From the details in the story, what conclusion can you draw about Ben's experience at The Clay Room?

 Ⓐ Working with clay was too difficult for him.

 Ⓑ He changed his mind about painting pottery.

 Ⓒ He liked painting pottery but preferred playing basketball.

 Ⓓ He liked painting the mug but didn't want to do it again.

12 How might this story have been different if it had taken place during an "open house," when many people would have been at The Clay Room?

 Ⓕ The story would have been exactly the same.

 Ⓖ Ben would not have been able to get as much help from Amy.

 Ⓗ Veronica would have been busy showing off.

 Ⓙ The kiln would not have been working.

13 **What is the theme of this story?**

Ⓐ You should always be interested in other people.

Ⓑ You can learn a lot by trying something new.

Ⓒ Facing your fears is the only way to get over them.

Ⓓ Trying different things is not always fun.

14 **What did Veronica and Ben do just *after* they chose the pieces they wanted to paint?**

Ⓕ They picked the colors they wanted to use.

Ⓖ They began painting.

Ⓗ They made the pieces out of clay.

Ⓙ They chose their designs.

15 **What event brought The Clay Shop to Ben's attention?**

Ⓐ He noticed a funny design on the bottom of a bowl.

Ⓑ Veronica introduced him to Amy, who runs the shop.

Ⓒ He broke his mug and needed a new one.

Ⓓ He saw the pretty pieces in the shop's display window.

16 **"One mug was *adorned* with a beautiful green and blue mosaic decoration." The word *adorned* means**

Ⓕ fired.

Ⓖ ruined.

Ⓗ decorated.

Ⓙ jeweled.

Directions: Read these two poems about rain. Then answer Questions 17–24.

The Rain Has Silver Sandals

by May Justus

The rain has silver sandals

For dancing in the spring,

And shoes with golden tassels

For summer's frolicking.

Her winter boots have hobnails

Of ice from heel to toe,

Which now and then she changes

For moccasins of snow.

from *Rain in Summer*

by Henry Wadsworth Longfellow

How beautiful is the rain!

After the dust and heat,

In the broad and fiery street,

In the narrow lane,

How beautiful is the rain!

How it clatters along the roofs,

Like the tramp of hoofs

How it gushes and struggles out

From the throat of the overflowing spout!

Across the window-pane

It pours and pours;

And swift and wide,

With a muddy tide,

Like a river down the gutter roars

The rain, the welcome rain!

Go On ➡

17 What is the poets' purpose for writing "The Rain Has Silver Sandals" and "Rain in Summer"?

Ⓐ to entertain people with funny things that happen in the rain

Ⓑ to explain important information about rain

Ⓒ to describe rain and what it's like

Ⓓ to persuade the reader that getting wet on rainy days is fun

18 How are "The Rain Has Silver Sandals" and "Rain in Summer" alike?

Ⓕ Both poems tell about rain changing into snow.

Ⓖ Both poems use the movement of feet to describe the rain.

Ⓗ Both poems describe rain clouds.

Ⓙ Both poems compare rain to a river.

19 Which answer *best* fits in Circle 1?

Ⓐ dancing

Ⓑ frolicking

Ⓒ tramps of hoofs

Ⓓ moccasins of snow

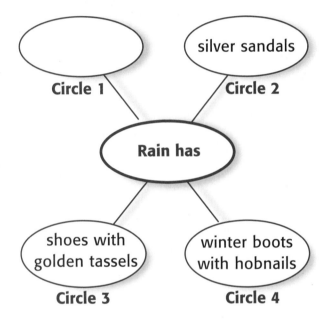

20 What is the theme of the two poems?

Ⓕ Watching rain can be an enjoyable experience.

Ⓖ Rain is a destructive force of nature.

Ⓗ Rain can make a person sad.

Ⓙ Rain is good for plants and trees.

21 From the details in "Rain in Summer," you can conclude that

Ⓐ rain is unenjoyable.

Ⓑ rain makes people sad.

Ⓒ the rain was welcome.

Ⓓ playing in the rain is fun.

22 In "The Rain Has Silver Sandals," the poet describes the rain's summer footwear as

Ⓕ shoes with golden tassels.

Ⓖ shoes with golden wings.

Ⓗ winter boots with hobnails.

Ⓙ silver sandals.

23 What is one way you can tell that "Rain in Summer" is a poem?

Ⓐ It gives facts about a real event.

Ⓑ It explains how rain causes flooding.

Ⓒ It is about a made-up place and event.

Ⓓ It rhymes.

24 "How it clatters along the roofs,/Like the *tramp* of hoofs...." What does the word *tramp* mean in this poem?

Ⓕ hobo

Ⓖ dance

Ⓗ stomp

Ⓙ swing

Teotihuacán: City of the Gods

Probably the best-known pyramids are those in Egypt. However, if you travel about 30 miles northeast of Mexico City, you will find Teotihuacán (tay-oh-tee-wuh-KAHN), an ancient city containing many spectacular pyramids. *Teotihuacán* means "city of the gods." It was given this name by the Aztecs, a later Native American civilization, several hundred years after the city's fall. The Aztecs believed that only the gods could have built the massive structures that line the city's roads.

View of Teotihuacán

Scientists believe that the great civilization of Teotihuacán began about 200 B.C. The city was a religious, commercial, and cultural center that had a great influence on other civilizations for almost 1,000 years. At the height of the city's development, more than 100,000 people lived within its borders. It was not only the largest city in the Americas but one of the largest cities of the ancient world.

Teotihuacán was planned in a grid system that covered about eight square miles. The city has four important landmarks—the Avenue of the Dead, the Pyramid of the Sun, the Pyramid of the Moon, and the Pyramid of the Feathered Serpent.

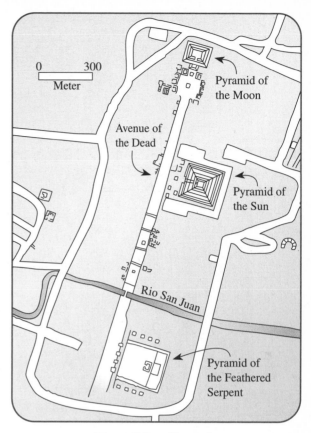

Map of Teotihuacán

Running through the center of the city is the Avenue of the Dead. The three-mile-long avenue varies in width from 40 to 95 yards. On both sides of the avenue are the major pyramids, palaces, and temples. It is thought that the builders of these structures placed them according to the positions of the sun, the moon, and the planets. Stone apartment compounds in the shape of pyramids also lined the avenue. Many families could live in these buildings, which were decorated with paintings, murals, and stone sculptures. These decorations are among the most beautiful of the ancient world. Running underneath the avenue was a drainage channel, it collected rainwater from neighboring streets and carried it to the San Juan River.

The Pyramid of the Sun, a massive pyramid, dominates the skyline of Teotihuacán. It is one of the largest structures ever built by Native Americans. Located on the east side of the Avenue of the Dead, the pyramid is 210 feet tall. Each of the four sides of its base

Go On ➡

Carving from the Pyramid of the Feathered Serpent

measures almost 700 feet in length. During excavation, a cave was discovered under the pyramid. It is thought that the cave may have been used for religious rituals.

At the northern end of the Avenue of the Dead is the Pyramid of the Moon. The pyramid was the site of religious ceremonies. Its top lined up exactly with the top of the mountain behind it. The ancient people who lived in Teotihuacán believed that pyramids represented sacred mountains.

The Pyramid of the Feathered Serpent lies in the southeastern end of the city. It is the most striking of all the pyramids. It sides are decorated with carvings of sacred images and more than 350 sculpted heads. Over half of these sculptures depict serpents with feathered headdresses. Because of the large number of graves found at this site, scientists believe the pyramid was used for sacrificial burials.

Unfortunately, the people of Teotihuacán did not have a writing system, so they left no written records. It is difficult to know what a typical day in that city was like. However, judging from the remains of the city, it is clear that many people were master artisans and craftspeople. This can be seen from the sculptures, murals, paintings, and ceramics they left behind. The remains of a large marketplace are evidence that the city was also a major trading center for the region. More than half the population were farmers. Each day they would leave Teotihuacán to work in the fields surrounding the city.

Though scientists know much about the city and its people, much about what life there was like is still a mystery. Just as puzzling is the city's sudden end. About 700 A.D., people stopped living in the city. No one knows for sure why they left or what happened to them. There is evidence that a great fire raged through the city at about this time. Some scientists believe that an invading army started the fire. Whatever the cause, the city and its people never recovered.

Today, scientists continue to excavate the ruins and study their findings. Slowly, they are finding pieces to this mystery. Maybe one day we will be able to understand fully this ancient people and their magnificent city.

Go On ➡

Ceremonial mask from Teotihuacán

25 What is the author's purpose in writing this article?

Ⓐ to persuade the reader to visit Mexico

Ⓑ to describe the city of Teotihuacán

Ⓒ to describe the Egyptian pyramids

Ⓓ to explain the importance of Aztec art

26 You can tell that "Teotihuacán: City of the Gods" is a nonfiction article because

Ⓕ it is about made-up characters and events.

Ⓖ it teaches a lesson about ancient people.

Ⓗ it gives facts and information about a real place.

Ⓙ it is about the past.

27 Which of the following statements is an *opinion*?

Ⓐ The Pyramid of the Sun is 210 feet tall.

Ⓑ Teotihuacán was the trading center of the region.

Ⓒ Running through the center of the city is the Avenue of the Dead.

Ⓓ These decorations are among the most beautiful of the ancient world.

28 Scientists do not know much about the people of Teotihuacán because

Ⓕ the Aztecs destroyed Teotihuacán.

Ⓖ they were craftspeople and artisans.

Ⓗ the city was a trading center.

Ⓙ the people left no written records.

29 This article is *mostly* about

Ⓐ the ancient city of Teotihuacán and its pyramids.

Ⓑ the Aztecs.

Ⓒ religious beliefs of ancient people.

Ⓓ the farmers of Teotihuacán.

30 Which detail from the article *best* supports the main idea of the article?

Ⓕ Scientists continue to excavate the ruins and study their findings.

Ⓖ About 700 A.D., people stopped living in the city.

Ⓗ The Pyramid of the Sun dominates the skyline of Teotihuacán.

Ⓘ The best-known pyramids are found in Egypt.

31 From the article, you can infer, or guess, that Teotihuacán

Ⓐ was supported by taxes on its people.

Ⓑ was a small village.

Ⓒ did not have water to put out fires.

Ⓓ was a well-developed, prosperous city.

32 "The Pyramid of the Sun, a *massive* pyramid, dominates the skyline of Teotihuacán." The word *massive* means

Ⓕ small.

Ⓖ carved.

Ⓗ huge.

Ⓘ painted.

STOP

Gators!

> **wetland:** marshy land; land where there is much moisture in the soil. Wetlands are important to the survival of many animals and plants and to the food chain of which they are part.

Scientists have learned a lot about the American alligator. They know that alligators are an important part of the **wetland** environment in the southeastern United States. To save alligators, scientists study them to learn more about how and where they live.

Alligators are reptiles, which means that they are cold-blooded animals. The body temperature of a cold-blooded animal depends on the temperature of the surrounding air. If an alligator is too cold, it cannot move very quickly. It must search for a warmer place. If it is too warm, it will move to a cooler place to lower its body temperature. By using the air temperature around them, alligators are able to control their body temperature.

Alligators, or gators, are nocturnal. They are active at night. They are also carnivorous. Gators love to eat meat. They eat turtles, snakes, and other small animals. When gators float at the water's edge, they look like brown logs. Only their eyes and nostrils, or noses, show above the water.

When an animal comes to the water's edge to drink, the gator

Adult alligators are on the average 6 to 8 feet long.

swings its powerful tail, knocking the prey into the water. The gator's sharp teeth lock around the prey and drag it under the water. The gator drowns larger victims before it tears them into pieces and swallows them.

An alligator hatchling

Gators use their claws and long snouts to dig burrows at the edge of the water. These burrows are called "gator holes." Gators use these holes to store uneaten food, hide from danger, and hibernate during cold weather.

Female alligators make a mound of mud and sticks that they use as a nest in wetland areas. They lay between forty and seventy hard-shelled eggs in the nest. The hatchlings, or baby alligators, are about six inches long. Raccoons, otters, birds, and snakes eat most of them. Only a few hatchlings survive to become adults.

Adult gators have few enemies, except for humans. At one time, hunters killed them for their meat and hide, or skin. Alligator hide was used to make leather for shoes, wallets, and other items. These items were very popular for a while.

Because of hunting, alligators were in danger of becoming **extinct**. In 1967, the United States government added alligators to the endangered species list. Laws were passed to stop people from hunting gators. This saved the American alligator. Today, they are no longer endangered. However, people must continue to protect alligators. They are important to the survival of the wetland environment.

extinct: no longer existing

B

Go On ➡

Question 1 This question is about **identifying the main idea** of an article.

STRATEGIES AND TIPS Identifying the Main Idea

- The **main idea** is what an article is mostly about. It tells you *who* or *what* the subject, or topic, of the selection is. The American alligator is the subject of the article "Gators!" The article gives you facts and information about where and how this animal lives.

- Do not confuse details in the selection with the main idea. Details such as how female alligators build their nests, or how alligators catch their prey add interest and provide the reader with more facts. But these details are not the main idea.

1. This article is *mostly* about

Ⓐ	how alligators raise their young.	**Incorrect.** This is discussed briefly, but it is not the main idea.
Ⓑ	why alligators were endangered.	**Incorrect.** This detail is discussed in the article, but the article does not focus on it.
Ⓒ	how alligators live in their environment.	**Correct. This is the main idea of the article. Reread the first paragraph.**
Ⓓ	the effects of being a cold-blooded animal.	**Incorrect.** These effects are related to the main idea.

TRY IT! The main idea of "Gators!" is how alligators live in their environment. Write a new title for this article based on this main idea. Then explain why it is a good title.

Title: _____

_____

_____

B

PRACTICE Identifying the Main Idea

The **main idea** is what an article is mostly about. It is the most important idea in the article. The main idea tells you *who* or *what* the subject, or topic, of the selection is.

Read the following paragraph.

> Scientists who study dinosaurs believe that today's birds may be related to one group of dinosaurs. All the dinosaurs in this particular group had two feet with three toes on each foot, just as birds do. The necks of these dinosaurs and the necks of birds are also very similar. These dinosaurs built nests, laid eggs, and cared for their young, just as birds do. Scientists have also discovered dinosaur fossils with feathers!

Now answer these questions.

1. What is the subject of this paragraph?

_____

2. Underline the sentence that best states the main idea of the paragraph.

   a. Some dinosaurs acted like birds.

   b. A certain group of dinosaurs may have been related to today's birds.

   c. Scientists study dinosaurs to see how they lived.

3. Write a title for this paragraph that contains the main idea.

_____

B

Question 2 This question is about **identifying supporting details**.

STRATEGIES AND TIPS) Identifying Supporting Details

- **Supporting details** give information about the main idea. The author makes the main idea stronger by supporting it with details. Without supporting details, the main idea can be hard to understand. For example, the main idea of "Gators!" is how alligators live in their environment. The author supports this idea by describing how alligators capture their prey.

- Not all details support the main idea. Some give information about other things, people, or places mentioned in the article. Although these details may be interesting, they do not necessarily relate to or support the main idea.

2 Which detail *best* supports the main idea of the article?

Ⓕ Gators use their claws and long snouts to dig burrows at the edge of the water.

Correct. This detail gives information about how alligators live in the wetland environment.

Ⓖ Alligator hide was used to make shoes and wallets.

Incorrect. This is a minor detail from the article. It does not support the main idea.

Ⓗ In 1967, the United States government added alligators to the endangered species list.

Incorrect. This is an important detail, but it does not relate to the main idea.

Ⓙ The hatchlings are about six inches long.

Incorrect. This fact appears in the article, but it does not support the main idea.

TRY IT! **Read the three details below. Underline the sentence that best supports the main idea: *How alligators live in their environment.***

1. Many people hunt alligators for their meat and their hides.

2. Female alligators build nests of sticks and mud.

3. Today, alligators are not endangered.

PRACTICE Identifying Supporting Details

Authors use **supporting details** to give more information about the main idea. These supporting details help the reader understand the main idea.

Read the following passage from a travel magazine. Look for details that support the main idea.

Saguaro cacti are found only in the Sonoran Desert of Arizona and northern Mexico. Fully grown, these beautiful cacti are tall and stately. The most interesting thing about them is that they can live for 200 years.

As a tiny seedling, the cactus takes root under a tree or bush. The tree acts as a "nurse plant," shading the tiny cactus from the harsh sun, winter freezes, and desert animals. At the age of 15, the cactus is only about 3 inches tall. As the saguaro grows, the nurse plant gradually dies.

When it is seventy-five years old, a saguaro is about 15 feet tall. Then it begins to grow its first "arm." Saguaros that are 150 years old may have several arms. By the time a saguaro reaches the age of 200, it can be more than 75 feet tall and can weigh several tons.

The main idea of the passage is written below. Fill in the rest of the chart with supporting details from the passage. The first one is done for you.

Main Idea:	Saguaro cacti go through many stages during their 200-year lives.
Detail:	As a tiny seedling, the cactus takes root under a tree or bush.
Detail:	
Detail:	

B

Question 3 This question is about **drawing conclusions**.

STRATEGIES AND TIPS Drawing Conclusions

- When you **draw a conclusion,** you make a judgment or decision based on the details in the selection. A conclusion is never a wild guess. From the details in the article you just read, you can draw the conclusion that scientists have learned a lot about how alligators survive in their environment.

- After you have drawn a conclusion, go back to the selection. Check the details. Make sure that they support your conclusion.

3 **Which detail supports the conclusion that laws have helped alligators survive?**

Ⓐ People must continue to protect alligators.

Incorrect. This detail appears in the article, but it does not support the conclusion.

Ⓑ Only a few hatchlings survive to become adults.

Incorrect. This sentence tells about baby alligator survival. It is not related to the conclusion.

Ⓒ Today, alligators are no longer endangered.

Correct. The laws have protected alligators, which today are no longer endangered. Reread the last paragraph in the article.

Ⓓ Raccoons, otters, birds, and snakes eat most of the baby alligators.

Incorrect. This may be an interesting detail, but it does not relate to the laws that were passed.

TRY IT! **List one detail from the article that supports this conclusion:** *Alligators are good at surprising and catching their prey.*

_____

_____

B

 **PRACTICE** **Drawing Conclusions**

When you **draw a conclusion,** you make a decision based on the information you have read in an article.

Read the following passage about alligators.

Alligators are showing up in some unexpected places. As people move into what was once alligator territory and build new communities, alligator sightings are becoming more common. People see alligators in their backyards, in parks, and on golf courses.

Living where alligators can be found poses dangers to people. After all, the alligators are wild animals. They have been known to attack people swimming in ponds and lakes. They have also been known to attack people's pets.

Sometimes people try to capture the alligators and take them to more remote locations, where they can once again live in the wild. Unfortunately, these places are becoming harder and harder to find.

What conclusion can you draw about why people are facing new dangers with alligators?

_____

_____

List two details from the passage that support your conclusion.

1. _____

_____

2. _____

_____

B

Question 4 This question is about **identifying sequence**.

STRATEGIES AND TIPS Identifying Sequence

- **Sequence** is the order in which events in an article occur. Sequence helps the reader understand what happens at the beginning, in the middle, and at the end of a selection. Authors often include words that signal time, such as *before, after, then, next,* and *finally*.

- Authors sometimes organize their writing around ideas rather than time. For example, in "Gators!" the author first writes about alligators being reptiles, and then about how they capture their prey. Then, the author discusses how alligators dig holes, and so on.

4 **What does a female alligator do *after* she makes a mound of mud and sticks?**

Ⓕ She knocks her prey into the water.

Incorrect. This event has no connection to her making the mound.

Ⓖ She moves to a cooler place to lower her body temperature.

Incorrect. This happens if the air temperature gets too warm.

Ⓗ She lays between forty and seventy eggs in the nest.

Correct. Read paragraph 6. After a female alligator builds a nest, she lays eggs.

Ⓙ She waits and listens for the baby alligators to hatch.

Incorrect. This is not mentioned in the article.

TRY IT! **Skim the article for facts about how alligators kill their prey. Write the correct sequence of details on the lines below.**

1. _____

2. _____

3. _____

B

PRACTICE Identifying Sequence

Sequence is the order in which events or ideas occur in an article.

Read the paragraph. Look for time words that signal sequence.

In the 1940s, alligator bags, shoes, and wallets were the height of fashion. Everyone wanted items made of alligator hides. In the years that followed, hunters killed thousands of alligators to meet the demands of manufacturers. Then, environmentalists pointed out just how important alligators were to the wetland environment. After that, lawmakers passed laws to protect alligators. No one could hunt them anymore. Now, alligators are no longer in danger of becoming extinct.

Circle the words that signal sequence in the paragraph. Record the sequence of events in the chart. The first event is done for you.

In the 1940s, alligator bags, shoes, and wallets were the height of fashion.

⬇

⬇

⬇

B

INSTRUCTION FOR GATORS!

STRATEGIES AND TIPS Classifying

- **Classifying** is grouping similar things together. You should be able to classify, or group together, similar ideas that go with the topic. For example, if the topic of an article is "wetlands animals," you might look for information in the article about snakes, alligators, birds, and turtles. These can be grouped together, or classified, as wetlands animals.

- You may want to use a chart to keep track of similar facts and details.

5 **Which answer *best* fits in Circle 1?**

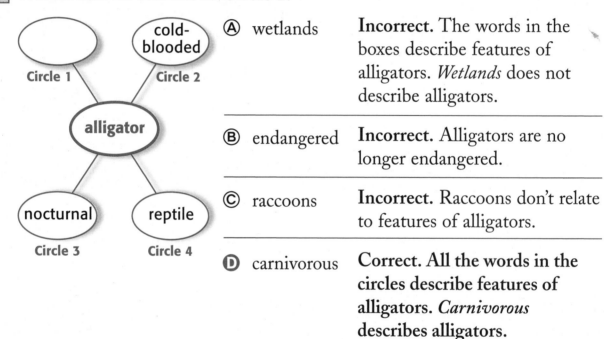

ⓐ wetlands   **Incorrect.** The words in the boxes describe features of alligators. *Wetlands* does not describe alligators.

ⓑ endangered   **Incorrect.** Alligators are no longer endangered.

ⓒ raccoons   **Incorrect.** Raccoons don't relate to features of alligators.

ⓓ carnivorous   Correct. All the words in the circles describe features of alligators. *Carnivorous* describes alligators.

TRY IT! **Skim the article for other animals that live in the southeastern wetlands. List four animals that eat baby alligators.**

_____ _____

_____ _____

B

PRACTICE Classifying

To **classify**, you group objects or ideas that are similar. You can better understand a topic if you can classify ideas and information about that topic.

Read the following passage from a white-water rafting brochure. Think about the items it mentions.

When you go white-water rafting with us, you can leave anything fancy at home. Pack clothes that are comfortable and tough. Bring T-shirts and shorts for warm days, and a parka for cold nights. There's no need to pack waterproof clothing for daywear, as it will be supplied.

As far as food goes, you need not bring anything because we will supply it all. Of course, if you have a favorite snack, you can bring a small amount. Make sure it's nothing that will spoil, especially if it gets wet.

A compass and binoculars are not necessary, as the tour provides these. But be sure to bring your own sun protection, such as a broad-brimmed hat, sunblock, and sunglasses.

With advance preparation, you'll be ready to have a great time!

What two categories of items must you take on the trip? Name each column. Then list the items in each group.

Category: _____   Category: _____

_____   _____

_____   _____

_____   _____

_____   _____

B

Question 6 This question is about **identifying cause and effect.**

STRATEGIES AND TIPS Identifying Cause and Effect

- A **cause** is why something happens. An **effect** is the result of what happens. You will not always find clue words to signal cause-and-effect relationships. Sometimes you have to infer the causes and effects.

- Often the cause is stated first: *Because laws protect gators, they are no longer in danger.* Other times the effect comes first: *Many gator babies do not make it to adulthood because they are eaten by other animals.*

6 **Because alligators are cold-blooded, they**

Ⓕ have poor eyesight.

Incorrect. This does not explain the effect, or result, of being cold-blooded.

Ⓖ tear their prey to pieces before swallowing them.

Incorrect. This does not explain the effect of being cold-blooded. There are cold-blooded animals that do not tear their prey to pieces.

Ⓗ float at the water's edge.

Incorrect. This is not a cause-and-effect statement. It does not explain the effect of being cold-blooded.

Ⓙ use the air temperature to control their body temperature.

Correct. Because alligators are cold-blooded (cause), they use the air temperature to control their body temperature (effect).

TRY IT! **Underline the cause and circle the effect in each sentence. The first one is done for you.**

1. Hunters used to kill alligators for their hide. As a result, alligators became endangered.

2. Because they are nocturnal, alligators generally are active at night.

3. Alligators can look like floating logs, so they may surprise their prey.

B

A **cause** is the reason why something happens. An **effect** is the result of what happens. You can find examples of cause and effect in almost anything you read. When you look for cause and effect, think about how one event leads to another. Often, one cause can have several effects.

Read the article below. As you read, think about causes and effects in the article.

It's a Bear's Life

Because of the unusual heat earlier this summer, Pequod and Paula, our city zoo's polar bears, were having a harder time than usual. Sometimes they seemed tired and listless. Other times they were just downright grumpy.

Zookeepers had to find creative ways to improve the bears' lives. Not only did the keepers find ways to keep Pequod and Paula cool but they also kept them entertained at the same time. Zookeepers froze the fish that Pequod and Paula eat in blocks of ice. The bears had to get through the ice to reach the tasty food. The zookeepers also put a huge block of ice right in bears' pool. The bears had fun pushing it around while they kept cool.

Write three causes and three effects from the article.

Causes: _____

_____

_____

Effects: _____

_____

_____

B

INSTRUCTION FOR GATORS!

STRATEGIES AND TIPS Identifying Fact and Opinion

- A **fact** is a statement that can be proved by checking encyclopedias, nonfiction books, or other reference sources. *Alligators are cold-blooded reptiles.* This is a fact that you can prove by looking in an encyclopedia or a science book.

- An **opinion** is a statement that expresses what someone feels or thinks. It cannot be proved or disproved. *Alligators are fascinating animals.* This is an opinion. Some people may feel this way. Others may not.

7 Which of the following statements is an *opinion*?

Ⓐ	Alligators are the scariest animals in the water.	**Correct.** This is an opinion. Many people fear alligators, but some may fear sharks more than alligators.
Ⓑ	Only a few alligator hatchlings survive to become adults.	**Incorrect.** This is a fact. Skim paragraph 6
Ⓒ	Some people killed alligators for their meat.	**Incorrect.** This is a fact. Skim paragraph 7.
Ⓓ	Scientists have learned a lot about the American alligator.	**Incorrect.** Skim paragraph 1. This is a fact.

TRY IT! Think about what you have learned about alligators. On the lines below, write one fact from the article. Then write one opinion that you have about alligators based on what you have read.

Fact: _____

_____

Opinion: _____

_____

B

Remember, a **fact** can be proved; an **opinion** cannot. Articles are often a combination of facts and opinions. You need to be able to recognize the difference between a fact and an opinion; you do not have to accept or agree with an author's opinions.

Read these science journal entries. Underline each sentence that states a fact. Circle each sentence that expresses an opinion. The first one is done for you.

The blue whale is the largest known animal ever to have lived on sea or land. One blue whale can weigh nearly 200 tons. That's awfully heavy for an animal!

I saw some horseshoe crabs. Scientists believe they look much the same way they looked 135 million years ago. You should never eat a horseshoe crab because they taste terrible!

Read each pair of sentences. Write *F* next to the fact. Write *O* next to the opinion. The first one is done for you.

1. __**F**__ Alligator hide can be made into bags and shoes.

   _____ Alligator bags are really pretty.

2. _____ No one should hunt alligators.

   _____ In 1967, laws were passed to stop alligator hunting.

3. _____ For years, the state of Florida protected alligators.

   _____ Protecting alligators is a smart thing for people to do.

4. _____ Alligators float beneath the surface of the water to surprise their prey.

   _____ Alligators are nature's fiercest hunters.

INSTRUCTION FOR GATORS!

B

Question 8 This question is about **using context clues**.

STRATEGIES AND TIPS Using Context Clues

- **Context clues** are the words, phrases, or sentences around an unfamiliar word. These clues can help you understand the meaning of the unfamiliar word.

- Unfamiliar words can also be defined with a definition clue. Read these sentences: *Alligators are* carnivorous. *Gators love* to eat meat. The author tells you that a carnivorous animal is one that eats meat.

8 "Alligators, or gators, are *nocturnal*. They are active at night." The word *nocturnal* means

Ⓕ	active during the day.	**Incorrect.** Paragraph 3 says gators are active at night. This is the opposite meaning.
Ⓖ	active during the night.	**Correct. The author defines *nocturnal* by adding "active at night" in the next sentence.**
Ⓗ	plant eaters.	**Incorrect.** Use *plant eaters* in place of *nocturnal*. The sentence does not make sense.
Ⓙ	meat eaters.	**Incorrect.** Use *meat eaters* in place of *nocturnal*. The sentence does not make sense.

TRY IT! **On the line in each sentence, write the context clue that helps define the underlined word.**

full-grown   **baby alligators**

1. The <u>hatchlings</u>, or _____, are about six inches long.

2. Only a few hatchlings survive to become <u>adults</u>.

These _____ alligators can be as long as 18 feet.

Context clues are the words, phrases, and sentences that surround an unfamiliar word. These clues can help you figure out the meaning of the unfamiliar word.

Read the following groups of sentences. Circle the context clue that helps you understand the meaning of the underlined word. Then write a new sentence using the word to show that you understand its meaning.

1. Yesterday I helped Mom plant a shrub. In the spring, the small bush will have pretty pink blooms.

_____

_____

2. Rabbits can live in large warrens. Many tunnels often connect these underground burrows.

_____

_____

3. When the dog saw Dad, he sprinted across the lawn. I've never seen him run so fast.

_____

_____

4. The pod of dolphins was surprisingly playful. At first, we were a little afraid of such a large group of them.

_____

_____

5. Ann was astonished to learn that her friend could sing so well. It took several days for the surprise to wear off.

_____

_____

B

Something New

Friday after basketball practice, Veronica and I shared a bowl of popcorn at her house. When we had finished, I noticed a funny design "dancing" across the bottom of the bowl. Knowing Veronica as well as I do, I recognized her signature doodle—a pattern of swirls, stars, and basketballs. I asked her where she had gotten the bowl.

Veronica explained that she'd painted the bowl herself at a place called The Clay Room. She asked me if I wanted to try it. I have to admit, I didn't really want to go. Painting bowls sounded pretty boring to me. But after a while, she talked me into it.

The next day, Veronica and I set off for The Clay Room. When we arrived, we stood admiring the colorful pieces displayed in the window. One mug was adorned with a beautiful green and blue **mosaic** decoration.

> **mosaic:** a design with small colored squares

Inside, Veronica introduced me to Amy, who runs the shop. I explained that I had never painted pottery before because it had never interested me. "Well, Ben," replied Amy, "the best way to change your mind is to try it." Amy explained that the first step was to choose the pieces we wanted to make. I decided on a mug. Veronica chose a coin bank.

"The next step," Amy explained, "is to choose an image or design you'd like to paint on your piece." She ushered us to a table scattered

with stencils, or patterns, and books with design ideas. Here we chose our designs.

"Next, you choose the background color," said Amy. She showed us a group of bottles filled with pottery paints, or glazes. She explained that before the pieces are heated, or fired, the paints appear pale and chalky. As they are heated, the colors change and darken. You really have to use your imagination to picture the look of the finished piece.

Amy picked up a dish painted a wispy yellow to show the see-through look that results from one coat of paint. She then picked up a bright blue box. "For this look, you need to use three coats of paint," she said.

She rotated the box slightly to show a hardened bubble **marring** the surface. Amy explained, "This is what happens if you don't let the paint dry after each coat. Moisture becomes trapped between the layers." She explained that when such a piece is fired at 2,000 degrees in the **kiln**, the moisture boils and bubbles.

> **marring:** damaging or spoiling

> **kiln:** an oven used to bake or harden clay

After applying the base coat, it's time to paint the design. "Again," she said, "you have to be careful of the colors you use." She held up a plate on which a green moon floated on a background of midnight blue. It had an eerie effect. Amy explained that the moon had originally been bright yellow. "The painter forgot that glazes change color in the kiln," she explained. "When the plate was heated, the dark blue showed through the yellow, turning the moon green."

Veronica and I spent the afternoon working on our pieces. I sure found out one thing: Getting pottery painting right is quite a challenge! But it's lots of fun. All I have to do is to look at my new green mug with its bright yellow star to remember this.

Go On ➡

B

Question 9 This question is about **identifying cause and effect**.

STRATEGIES AND TIPS · Identifying Cause and Effect

- A **cause** is the reason why something happens. An **effect** is the result of what happens. Sometimes you will find clue words, such as *because* or *as a result,* that signal cause-and-effect relationships. When no clue words are used, you have to infer, or guess, the cause and effect.

- Often the cause is stated first. For example: *Because he thought painting pottery would be boring, Ben did not want to go to The Clay Room.* Other times the effect comes first. For example: *The color of the glaze darkens as a result of being fired in the kiln.*

9 Hardened bubbles mar the surface of a pot as a result of

Ⓐ	painting the design incorrectly.	**Incorrect.** This detail is not in the story.
Ⓑ	forgetting that glazes change colors in the kiln.	**Incorrect.** This does not explain *why* bubbles appear in the glaze.
Ⓒ	being careless with the colors you use.	**Incorrect.** This does not explain *why* there are bubbles in the finished piece.
Ⓓ	not waiting for the paint to dry after each coat.	**Correct.** Bubbles will appear in the glaze if you do not let it dry between coats.

TRY IT! **Underline the cause and circle the effect in each of the following sentences. The first one is done for you.**

1. The moon on one mug was green because the dark blue of the background showed through the yellow.

2. The colors of the glaze change and darken as a result of being heated.

3. Since I was new to pottery painting, I decided to start with something simple.

A **cause** is the reason why something happens. An **effect** is the result of what happens. When you look for cause and effect, think about how one event leads to another. Sometimes, one cause can have several effects.

Read this diary entry from a story. Look for cause-and-effect relationships as you read.

> Dear Diary,
>   The river flooded at 1:25 P.M. yesterday. Guess what? We have no school today. Lots of businesses and government offices are also closed. A spokesperson for the Emergency Flood Service made an announcement last night on the radio. She said that because of the unusual rains this summer, the river had already been near flood level. Apparently, the storm of the last two days put it over its banks. The raging waters caused the levee, the dirt wall that protects the town, to break. The water on Elm Street is so deep, that many people had to abandon their cars. Fortunately, no one was injured by the flood. And I got an unexpected holiday!

List three causes of the flood.

1. _____

2. _____

3. _____

List three effects of the flood.

1. _____

2. _____

3. _____

INSTRUCTION FOR SOMETHING NEW

B

Question 10 This question is about **comparing and contrasting**.

STRATEGIES AND TIPS Comparing and Contrasting

- **Comparing** is finding ways that people, events, things, or ideas are alike.
Contrasting is finding out how things are different. In the story, Amy contrasts
a dish painted with one coat with a box painted with three coats.

10 **How was Ben's mug different from the mug he saw in the window?**

F His mug had a bubbled glaze, but the one in the window didn't.

Incorrect. Ben's mug did not have bubbles in the glaze.

G The mug in the window sparkled, but his had a dull look.

Incorrect. These details do not appear in the story.

H The mug in the window had a blue and green mosaic pattern, but his was green with a yellow star.

Correct. These details are included in the third and last paragraphs of the story.

J His mug was easy to make, whereas the one in the window had been difficult to make.

Incorrect. There is no mention in the story about how easy or difficult it was to make either mug.

TRY IT! Veronica and Ben went to The Clay Room together. Compare the experience by describing how it was alike for each of them. Contrast the experience by describing how it was different.

1. Compare: _____

_____

2. Contrast: _____

_____

B

When **comparing,** authors may use words such as *alike, same, both,* and *similarly.* When **contrasting,** authors may use words such as *but, however, on the other hand,* and *different.*

Read the paragraph. As you read, look for words that signal comparing and contrasting.

I went to The Pottery Shed to make presents for my mom and dad. I chose mugs for both of them. Mom's favorite color is blue, so I painted the background of her mug blue. Then I decorated it with yellow flowers and green leaves. I did the background of Dad's mug just like Mom's. I decorated it, however, with brown footballs and green football jerseys. Both mugs came out great. They will be so surprised!

Circle words in the paragraph that signal comparing and contrasting. Fill in the chart below to show how the presents are alike and different.

Ways the Presents Are Alike	Ways the Presents Are Different

B

Question 11 This question is about **drawing conclusions**.

STRATEGIES AND TIPS Drawing Conclusions

- When you **draw a conclusion,** you make a judgment or decision based on the details you have read in a story. Since there is no mention in the story of making pottery—only painting it—you can draw the conclusion that Veronica and Ben did not make the pieces they painted.

- After you have drawn a conclusion, go back to the story. Check the details. Make sure that they support your conclusion.

11 From the details in the story, what conclusion can you draw about Ben's experience at The Clay Room?

Ⓐ Working with clay was too difficult for him.

Incorrect. There are no details in the story to support this conclusion.

Ⓑ He changed his mind about painting pottery.

Correct. In the beginning of the story, Ben thinks painting pottery is boring. By the end of the story, he thinks it is challenging and fun.

Ⓒ He liked painting pottery but preferred playing basketball.

Incorrect. We know that Ben plays basketball, but there are not enough details in the story to support this conclusion.

Ⓓ He liked painting the mug but didn't want to do it again.

Incorrect. There are no details in the story to support this conclusion.

TRY IT! List two details from the story that support this conclusion: *Amy is a skilled teacher when it comes to painting pottery.*

1. _____

2. _____

B

When you **draw a conclusion** about characters or events in a story, you make a decision or judgment based on the details you have read.

Read the following letter about a class project.

Dear Grandpa,
　　Our teacher decided that we should learn about fish. Everyone in the class groaned when we heard we'd be raising trout. Since then we have all changed our minds. First, we put the trout eggs in the tank and waited. When the trout hatched, we all cheered. It was so neat! We draw pictures of the fish as they grow. Every morning we all run over to the tank to see how they are doing. In a few weeks, we are going to release the trout into streams. We will miss our little friends, but it will be a happy day because they will be free.
　　Love,
　　Sara

What conclusion can you draw about how the class enjoys raising trout? Write it in the chart. Then list details from the letter that support your conclusion.

Conclusion:	
Detail 1:	
Detail 2:	
Detail 3:	

B

Question 12 This question is about **identifying the setting** of a story.

STRATEGIES AND TIPS   Identifying Setting

- The **setting** of a story is where and when the events of the story happen. The setting often affects what happens in the story. This story mostly takes place at The Clay Room on a Saturday. The equipment there and the instructor's explanations help make Ben's experience a successful one. If the place had been poorly equipped and so crowded that Ben could not have had Amy's attention, his experience might have been disappointing.

- When you read a story, ask yourself: *Where are the events in this story happening? When are these events happening? How does the setting affect what happens in the story?*

12 How might this story have been different if it had taken place during an "open house," when many people would have been at The Clay Room?

ⓕ The story would have been exactly the same.

Incorrect. The Clay Room would have been much more crowded for an "open house."

ⓖ Ben would not have been able to get as much help from Amy.

Correct. Amy would have needed to spend more time with other people who had come to find out about pottery painting.

ⓗ Veronica would have been busy showing off.

Incorrect. There is no mention that Veronica is a showoff.

ⓙ The kiln would not have been working.

Incorrect. The kiln would probably have been used by all of the people.

TRY IT!   Veronica and Ben go to The Clay Room by themselves. It must be near where they live—in a city or town. Suppose they lived on farms. How would that have changed the story?

_____

_____

_____

B

PRACTICE Identifying Setting

The **setting** of a story is the place and time in which a story occurs. The setting of a story can affect what happens in the plot.

Read this passage from a story. As you read, look for clues that tell you where and when the events take place. Then write your answers to the questions.

> "Cynthia Jones, come down from that tree *immediately*," Mama yelled from the kitchen.
>
> "She must have telescopes for eyes," Cindy said aloud. "How else would she know? I climbed up here so quietly."
>
> Cynthia eased herself down the enormous trunk. It was another hot, humid day with nothing to do. Some of the neighborhood crowd had walked into town to see Mr. Welles's new 1925 Oldsmobile. But Cynthia had already seen it twice, and it just made her jealous. Twenty-five years into the 20th century, her parents were still driving around in their horse and wagon.

1. Where does this story take place?

_____

2. What year is it?

_____

3. What time of the year is it?

_____

4. How do you think the setting will affect what happens in the story?

_____

B

Question 13 This question is about **understanding the theme** of a story.

STRATEGIES AND TIPS | Understanding Theme

- The **theme** is the message of a story. The theme often expresses a general statement about human nature or about life. The theme sometimes relates to a lesson the main character learns—or does not learn.

- When identifying the theme of a story, ask yourself: *What was the main character like at the beginning of the story? What was the character like at the end of the story? What lesson did he or she learn?*

13 **What is the theme of this story?**

Ⓐ You should always be interested in other people.

Incorrect. This may be true, but it does not express the theme of the story.

Ⓑ You can learn a lot by trying something new.

Correct. At first, Ben does not want to go to The Clay Room, but he ends up learning about pottery painting.

Ⓒ Facing your fears is the only way to get over them.

Incorrect. This message does not have anything to do with the events of the story.

Ⓓ Trying different things is not always fun.

Incorrect. On the contrary, Ben ended up trying something new and having fun.

TRY IT! **Skim the story to find three details that support this theme:** *Sometimes you can learn interesting things in unlikely places.*

Detail 1: _____

Detail 2: _____

Detail 3: _____

The **theme** is the message of a story. The theme sometimes relates to a lesson the main character learns—or does not learn.

Read the following story and answer the questions.

When Thea heard that her family was driving to the lake, she ran into her room, flopped on the bed, and sobbed. They had driven to the lake every weekend this summer. It was full of young couples with very young children and old couples with very young grandchildren. Nobody to play with and nothing to do. But Thea's parents stood firm. "You know how hard your father and I work all week," said her mother. "We need to get some peace and quiet on our days off."

When they finally arrived, Thea sat on a picnic bench, officially beginning her weekend of boredom. As she stared down the beach, a blue T-shirt suddenly came into view.

"Hi," said a voice. "I'm Jill." As Jill and Thea traded bits of information about their lives, Thea began to think that maybe this weekend wouldn't be as bad as she had thought.

Circle the theme of the story. On the lines below, explain why you chose that theme.

Theme 1: Sometimes the unexpected happens and makes life better.

Theme 2: Being selfish just causes problems.

_____

_____

_____

B

STRATEGIES AND TIPS Identifying Sequence

- **Sequence** is the order in which events in a story happen. As you read a story, look for words, such as *before, after, then, next,* and *finally,* that signal time. For example: *Amy explained that the first step was to choose the pieces we wanted to make.* The word *first* tells you that this is the thing people do first when they come to The Clay Room.

- Before you answer a question, read all the choices. Think back to the events. In your mind, try to put the events in order.

14 What did Veronica and Ben do just *after* they chose the pieces they wanted to paint?

(F) They picked the colors they wanted to use.

Incorrect. This was not the first thing that Veronica and Ben did after picking their pieces.

(G) They began painting.

Incorrect. This happened later.

(H) They made the pieces out of clay.

Incorrect. They did not have to make their own pieces. They were already made.

(J) They chose their designs.

Correct. Skim paragraph 5. This is the step that follows picking out a piece to paint.

TRY IT! These steps are out of sequence. Write them in the correct order. Use the words *first, next, then,* and *finally*.

Fire the piece in the kiln. Apply the background color to the piece. Choose a background color. Paint the design.

1. _____

2. _____

3. _____

4. _____

Sequence is the order in which events in a story happen. Sometimes, but not always, an author will use words that signal time.

INSTRUCTION FOR SOMETHING NEW

Read the following short story. As you read, circle the words that signal sequence.

> While I was visiting Grandma last summer, my parents redid my room. First, they moved all the furniture out. Then they took up the rug. They painted the room white with a blue trim. Then they put down a new blue rug. They moved the bed back in. As a final touch, Mom hung a poster of my favorite rock group over my bed. It was awesome!

Use the chart below to record the sequence of events in the story. The first event is done for you.

First, they moved all the furniture out.

↓

↓

↓

↓

↓

© 2004 Options Publishing, Inc.

B

Question 15 This question is about **identifying details** in a story.

STRATEGIES AND TIPS Identifying Details

- **Details** give the reader more information about the story. They help the reader organize information and keep events in order. Details give the reader information about *who* the story is about, *what* the story is about, *where* the story occurred, *when* the story occurred, *why* an event occurred, and *how* it occurred.

- When you are asked for information about a detail, do not reread the entire selection. Think about what detail you need to find and where in the story you are most likely to find it. Then skim that section to look for the information.

---

15 **What event brought The Clay Shop to Ben's attention?**

Ⓐ	He noticed a funny design on the bottom of a bowl.	**Correct.** His noticing Veronica's design got her talking about the shop, which, in turn, got Ben interested in it.
Ⓑ	Veronica introduced him to Amy, who runs the shop.	**Incorrect.** Veronica introduced Ben to Amy after he got to the shop.
Ⓒ	He broke his mug and needed a new one.	**Incorrect.** No mention is made in the story of Ben breaking a mug.
Ⓓ	He saw the pretty pieces in the shop's display window.	**Incorrect.** Veronica and Ben admired the pieces in the display window after Ben decided to visit The Clay Shop.

TRY IT! Skim for details in the story to help you answer the following questions.

1. What did Ben find amazing in the window of The Clay Shop?

_____

2. What did Ben's mug look like?

_____

PRACTICE Identifying Details

Details tell you more about people, places, things, and events. Details are the *who, what, when, where, why*, and *how* of what you read.

Read the following story about a school trip. Look for details.

One beautiful day in late September, Shonda's class went on a trip by school bus to the Lonesome Pines Environmental Center. The purpose of the trip was to learn about animals and the environment.

After a short talk at the visitors' hall, the class headed to the pond. The first animal Shonda saw was a beaver. It was swimming toward a pile of dried grass that looked like a haystack. Shonda knew it was a beaver lodge, because she had seen one in a book.

In the afternoon the class hiked along a trail through the woods. He told the class that there were bears in the area, but Shonda was glad *not* to come face to face with any.

Underline the details in the story that tell you *who, what, where, when, why,* and *how*. Then use the chart below to record the details.

Who is the main character?	
What did she do?	
Where did she go?	
When did she go?	
Why did she go?	
How did Shonda recognize the beaver lodge?	

B

Question 16 This question is about **using context clues**.

- **Context clues** are words, phrases, or sentences around an unfamiliar word.

- Read this sentence: *She explained that when such a piece is fired at 2,000 degrees in the kiln, the moisture boils and bubbles.* If you didn't know what a kiln was, you could figure out that since it is a place where pottery is fired, or heated, at 2,000 degrees, it must be a type of oven.

16 "One mug was *adorned* with a beautiful green and blue mosaic decoration." The word *adorned* means

Ⓕ	fired.	**Incorrect.** This answer does not make sense. *Firing* is the process by which the glaze is baked onto the mug.
Ⓖ	ruined.	**Incorrect.** This definition does not make sense in place of the word *adorned*.
Ⓗ	decorated.	**Correct.** The word *decoration* is a context clue.
Ⓙ	jeweled.	**Incorrect.** There are no clues to suggest that the mug is decorated with jewels.

TRY IT! Read each pair of sentences. Circle the context clues that help you figure out the meaning of the underlined word. Write the meaning of the word.

1. We <u>admired</u> the colorful pieces displayed in the window. I really liked the purple plate with white stripes.

_____

2. She <u>ushered</u> us to a table scattered with stencils. As she led us through the room, I noticed all kinds of pottery.

_____

PRACTICE **Using Context Clues**

Context clues are the words, phrases, and sentences around an unfamiliar word. These clues can help you figure out the meaning of the unfamiliar word.

Read the following sentences or pairs of sentences. Circle the context clues that help you understand the meaning of the underlined word. Then write a sentence using the word.

1. We stayed away from the kiln because of the <u>intense</u>, or extreme, heat.

_____

_____

2. The <u>glazes</u> were in bottles on a shelf. I chose several different colors to paint my pot.

_____

_____

3. <u>Fascinated</u> by stories of pottery making, I decided that my friends would also be interested in hearing them.

_____

_____

4. Many <u>ancient</u> cultures in the New World made pottery. People who lived long ago in the Southwest made wonderful designs.

_____

_____

5. Europeans were no strangers to <u>earthenware</u>. Pottery played an important part in their daily lives, too.

_____

_____

© 2004 Options Publishing, Inc.

The Rain Has Silver Sandals

by May Justus

The rain has silver sandals

For dancing in the spring,

And shoes with golden tassels

For summer's frolicking.

Her winter boots have hobnails

Of ice from heel to toe,

Which now and then she changes

For moccasins of snow.

from *Rain in Summer*

by Henry Wadsworth Longfellow

How beautiful is the rain!

After the dust and heat,

In the broad and fiery street,

In the narrow lane,

How beautiful is the rain!

How it clatters along the roofs,

Like the tramp of hoofs

How it gushes and struggles out

From the throat of the overflowing spout!

Across the window-pane

It pours and pours;

And swift and wide,

With a muddy tide,

Like a river down the gutter roars

The rain, the welcome rain!

Go On ➡

B

Question 17 This question is about **identifying the author's purpose**.

> **STRATEGIES AND TIPS**   Identifying Author's Purpose
>
> - The **author's purpose** is the reason an author writes a story, article, or poem. The purpose can be to *entertain, persuade, inform, explain,* or *describe.*
> - The author's purpose often relates to the theme of a poem or story. The theme is usually a general statement about human nature or about life. In "The Rain Has Silver Sandals" and "Rain in Summer," the poets portray rain in a positive way: Watching rain can be an enjoyable experience.

17 **What is the poets' purpose for writing "The Rain Has Silver Sandals" and "Rain in Summer"?**

Ⓐ to entertain people with funny things that happen in the rain

Incorrect. The poets do not describe funny things that happen in the rain.

Ⓑ to explain important information about rain

Incorrect. The poets do not give information about rain.

Ⓒ to describe rain and what it's like

Correct. The poets' purpose is to describe rain and what it's like.

Ⓓ to persuade the reader that getting wet on rainy days is fun

Incorrect. The poets do not include anything about getting wet on rainy days.

TRY IT!   Skim the poems to find three examples of words and phrases that suggest that the poets wanted to describe rain to the reader. Write them below.

1. _____

2. _____

3. _____

B

The most common purposes for writing are to *entertain, persuade, inform, explain,* or *describe.* Knowing the **author's purpose** for writing a selection can help you focus on what is important. An author may have more than one purpose for writing.

Read this story. Think about the author's purpose for writing.

It wasn't Kareem's idea to put raingear on the dog to go out in the rain. His little sister, Fanicia, insisted. "You have a raincoat, a rain hat, and boots. And so do I," she announced sternly. "So why shouldn't Duchess?"

Duchess crept over to sniff her new raingear as if it might be something to eat. Satisfied that it wasn't, she let out a little whimper as if to say, "Why did you bother to call me if this isn't something to eat?"

Duchess looked warily at Fanicia as she slipped the plaid boots over the dog's front paws. "There!" Fanicia said with triumph. "Two down, two to go."

But Duchess didn't wait for the other two boots. She took off down the steps, across the lawn, and down the sidewalk, running through a large puddle in front of the Brewsters' house.

What is the author's purpose for writing this story? List the purpose and two examples from the story that helped you decide.

Purpose: _____

Example: _____

Example: _____

INSTRUCTION FOR POETRY

B

Question 18 This question is about **comparing and contrasting**.

STRATEGIES AND TIPS Comparing and Contrasting

- **Comparing** is showing ways that things are alike. **Contrasting** is showing ways that things are different. In poetry, poets often compare and contrast things to describe them. In "The Rain Has Silver Sandals," for example, the poet compares rain to types of footwear or shoes.

- Sometimes you can find clue words in a poem that tell you things are being compared: *like, as,* or *is.* Clue words that signal contrast include *unlike* and *while.*

18 **How are "The Rain Has Silver Sandals" and "Rain in Summer" alike?**

Ⓕ Both poems tell about rain changing into snow.
Incorrect. Only the poem "The Rain Has Silver Sandals" mentions snow.

Ⓖ Both poems use the movement of feet to describe the rain.
Correct. "The Rain Has Silver Sandals" tells about dancing and frolicking. "Rain in Summer" tells about the tramps of hoofs.

Ⓗ Both poems describe rain clouds.
Incorrect. Neither poem mentions rain clouds.

Ⓙ Both poems compare rain to a river.
Incorrect. The poem "Rain in Summer" compares rain to a river, but "The Rain Has Silver Sandals" does not.

TRY IT! Read the last stanza of "Rain in Summer" again. Find the lines in which the poet compares rain to a river. Write two examples of how rain and a river are alike.

1. _____

2. _____

B

When authors **compare** people, events, things, or ideas, they describe how they are alike. When authors **contrast** people, events, things, or ideas, they describe how they are different.

Read the story. Look for examples of comparing and contrasting.

I'll never forget the first summer I went to visit Aunt Lucy. I was used to a few geraniums in the window box that my mom planted every year. Other than that, I hardly paid flowers any mind.

Aunt Lucy had a huge garden full of colorful flowers. Boy, did some of them smell good! I liked them all, but my two favorites became the lilies and the petunias.

Lilies are tall, skinny plants that grow from bulbs. Aunt Lucy had orange ones with spots that stood in a big clump in the middle of the lawn. She said that they came in other colors as well. When they bloomed, I cut some and put them in a vase.

The petunias are small plants that grow from seeds. They lined the path to Aunt Lucy's back door. They were all different colors and didn't have much of a stem, so we couldn't cut them to put in a vase. But that was okay. We were just happy seeing them every day.

Fill in the chart to compare and contrast lilies and petunias.

How Lilies and Petunias Are Alike	How Lilies and Petunias Are Different

Question 19 This question is about **classifying,** or grouping things together.

STRATEGIES AND TIPS Classifying

- **Classifying** is grouping similar things or details together. In "The Rain Has Silver Sandals," the poet describes the rain as having "silver sandals for dancing in the spring." As you read the rest of the poem, you find details that describe what kinds of shoes the rain wears during other seasons. These types of shoes can be grouped together, or classified.

19 **Which answer *best* fits in Circle 1?**

Ⓐ dancing — **Incorrect.** The words in the circles describe types of shoes.

Ⓑ frolicking — **Incorrect.** *Frolicking* tells what the rain does in the summer.

Ⓒ tramps of hoofs — **Incorrect.** *Tramps of hoofs* is a description from the other poem, "Rain in Summer."

Ⓓ moccasins of snow — **Correct.** Moccasins are a type of shoe.

TRY IT! **In each group of words, cross out the one item that does not belong with the others. Then write a title for each group that tells what the items have in common.**

1. summer, spring, vacation, winter

   _____

2. loses, gushes, pours, overflows

   _____

B

To **classify,** you group objects or ideas that are similar. You can better understand a topic if you can categorize ideas and information about that topic.

INSTRUCTION FOR POETRY

Read the selection. Think about the topic. Look for ideas and details that can be grouped together.

In summer, Francesca and her friends look forward to having free time for the activities they love. When the weather is nice, they like to be on the move. They can roller-blade for hours in the park or ride bicycles along its special paths. They even look forward just to going to one another's house or to the store. That's because they jump on a scooter or skateboard to get there.

Rainy days change Francesca and her friends' outdoor activities. But there is still a lot to do indoors. They brave the raindrops to get together to play board games. If the weather is really bad, they might curl up at home with their favorite book or get out their drawing and painting supplies. Of course, if Francesca and her friends run out of things to do, they can always clean their rooms!

Now fill in the chart.

Topic: Outdoor Activities	Topic: Indoor Activities

B

Question 20 This question is about **understanding theme** in poetry.

> ### STRATEGIES AND TIPS Understanding Theme
>
> - The **theme** is the main message of a selection. A theme often expresses a general statement about human nature or about life.
>
> - When you are given a choice of themes on a test, make sure you understand what the statements mean. Then ask yourself which statement, or message, best tells about them.

20 **What is the theme of the two poems?**

F Watching rain can be an enjoyable experience.

Correct. Both poets describe the rain in positive ways. Longfellow describes rain as beautiful, whereas Justus describes how rain looks in different seasons.

G Rain is a destructive force of nature.

Incorrect. Neither poem portrays rain as being destructive.

H Rain can make a person sad.

Incorrect. Both poets describe rain as a happy experience, not a sad one.

J Rain is good for plants and trees.

Incorrect. Neither poem mentions rain as being good for plants and trees.

TRY IT! **Reread both poems. Find three details that support the theme:** *Watching rain can be enjoyable.*

1. _____

2. _____

3. _____

 **PRACTICE** **Understanding Theme**

The **theme** is the message or lesson of a poem or a story. A theme often expresses a general statement about human nature or about life.

Read the following story. As you read, think about its theme.

> Tanya and Jan were best friends. They walked to and from school together each day. They had lunch together and shared their thoughts with each other. Both girls played on the same basketball team. They were as close as friends could be.
>
> When Jan received an invitation to Laura's birthday party, she was surprised to learn that Tanya hadn't been invited. Laura was popular, and her party was bound to be a lot of fun. Jan really wanted to go to the party, but she knew Tanya would be hurt if she did. She and Tanya always went to the movies together on Saturdays.
>
> On Friday, Jan said to Tanya, "I'll pick you up at noon tomorrow."
>
> "I thought you were going to Laura's party," said Tanya.
>
> "No, I decided to skip it," said Jan. "Some things are more important."

Circle the theme of the story. Then, write three details from the story that support that theme.

Theme 1: Friendship can be more important than having fun.

Theme 2: Friendships sometimes involve hard work.

Detail 1: _____

Detail 2: _____

Detail 3: _____

B

Question 21 This question is about **drawing conclusions** from a poem.

STRATEGIES AND TIPS Drawing Conclusions

- When you **draw a conclusion,** you make a judgment or decision based on the details you have read in a poem or story. In "The Rain Has Silver Sandals," the poet describes rain with different shoes for each season. You can conclude that she wants you to see how rain can be different.

- After you have drawn a conclusion, go back to the poem or story. Check the details and make sure they support your conclusion.

21 **From the details in "Rain in Summer," you can conclude that**

Ⓐ	rain is unenjoyable.	**Incorrect.** There are no details in the poem to suggest that rain is unenjoyable. Just the opposite is true.
Ⓑ	rain makes people sad.	**Incorrect.** There are no details in the poem to suggest that rain makes people sad.
Ⓒ	the rain was welcome.	**Correct.** In the last line, the poet writes, "The rain, the welcome rain!"
Ⓓ	playing in the rain is fun.	**Incorrect.** The poet does not mention playing in the rain, just watching the rain.

TRY IT! **Which two details from "The Rain Has Silver Sandals" might lead you to conclude that the poet lived in a climate with big differences in seasons?**

1. _____

2. _____

When you **draw a conclusion** about a character or event in a poem or story, you make a decision or judgment based on the details you have read.

Read the following poem to see how the poet describes rain.

One Rainy Morning
by Trey Fernandez

I woke up to the sound of rain
Tap-dancing on my windowpane.
Of all the days for clouds to burst,
This surely was the very worst.

My brother Felix, with his bike,
Was going riding with pal Mike.
My sister, Gina, camping out
Last night, will come home soaked, no doubt.

And as for me, I had big plans,
To hit home runs and thrill the fans.
Instead of pleasing baseball lovers—
I guess I'll just pull up the covers.

What conclusion can you draw about rain from this poem? Write it in the chart. Then list two details that support your conclusion.

Conclusion:
Detail 1:
Detail 2:

B

Question 22 This question is about **identifying details** in a poem.

Identifying Details

- **Details** give the reader more information about a poem. They help you organize the information and keep events in order. Details tell you the **5Ws and H.** They tell you *who, what, when, where, why,* and *how.*

- When you are asked for information about a detail, think about where in the poem you are most likely to find it. Then skim that section to look for the information.

22 In "The Rain Has Silver Sandals," the poet describes the rain's summer footwear as

F shoes with golden tassels.

Correct. Reread lines 3 and 4 of the poem. The poet states that the rain has shoes with golden tassels for summer's frolicking.

G shoes with golden wings.

Incorrect. The shoes have golden tassels, not wings.

H winter boots with hobnails.

Incorrect. This answer describes winter footwear. The rain would not wear boots with hobnails in the summer.

J silver sandals.

Incorrect. This is the footwear that rain wears in the spring.

TRY IT! Look for details in "Rain in Summer" that help you answer the following questions.

1. How does the rain travel from the spout?

_____

2. Where does the rain pour "swift and wide, with a muddy tide"?

_____

B

Details are the *who, what, when, where, why,* and *how* of what you read. Details tell you more about people, places, things, and events.

Read the beginning of a story below. Look for details that tell *who, what, when, where, why,* **and** *how*.

> On Thursday, Tanika and Kobe's teacher, Ms. Rodriguez, asked the students to work in pairs and draw a strange animal. The drawing had to be as realistic as possible. Some students drew spiders. One pair tried to draw a cockroach. Kobe and Tanika had an even better idea.
>
> Saturday, they got on a downtown bus with Tanika's older brother Bernie. They had pencils and paper with them. Their destination was the Natural History Museum. There, they could see some real dinosaur skeletons. They knew that they could make a great drawing. They did not know, however, the strange adventure that awaited them in the Hall of Bones.

Answer the questions in the chart below.

Who are the main characters?	
What do they have to do?	
Where are they going?	
How are they traveling?	

B

Question 23 This question is about **identifying genre**.

STRATEGIES AND TIPS Identifying Genre

- **Genre** is the type of literature you read, such as *stories, folktales, informational articles,* or *poetry*.

- Some literature gives you facts about real people, places, events, and things. *Articles, biographies,* and *autobiographies* are nonfiction genres. *Folktales, legends,* and *realistic fiction* tell stories. They are fiction genres.

- *Poetry* is written in rhythmic lines rather than in sentences. Poems use colorful language and imagery to communicate a feeling. Many poems are rhymed—they repeat syllable sounds at the ends of paired lines. The poem "The Rain Has Silver Sandals" expresses a certain feeling in just a few lines.

23 **What is one way you can tell that "Rain in Summer" is a poem?**

Ⓐ It gives facts about a real event.

Incorrect. Although this event may have happened to the poet, this does not classify it as a poem.

Ⓑ It explains how rain causes flooding.

Incorrect. Many types of writing can explain how rain causes flooding.

Ⓒ It is about a made-up place and event.

Incorrect. The poem may be about a made-up place and event, but this alone does not make it a poem.

Ⓓ It rhymes.

Correct. "Rain in Summer" is written in lines that rhyme.

TRY IT! **Read "The Rain Has Silver Sandals" again. List characteristics of the selection that classify it as poetry.**

_____

_____

B

Genre is the type of literature you read, such as *poetry, folktales, myths, legends, short stories,* and books about people, places, and events that are made up. These are fictional genres. *Articles, essays, biographies,* and other books about real people, places, and events are nonfiction genres.

Read each of the following passages. Decide which genre the passage represents and circle the correct answer. Write one clue that helped you identify the genre.

1. Chip slowly opened the door in the tree. He peered in. It looked safe, so he stepped in carefully. Suddenly the ground below him gave way. Chip found himself sliding down a long and winding tunnel. At the end of it, he hit a hard floor with a clunk!

informational article   story   poem

Clue: _____

2. The hot sand
burns my feet.
I'll jump in the water
to beat the heat.

informational article   story   poem

Clue: _____

Question 24 This question is about **using context clues**.

STRATEGIES AND TIPS Using Context Clues

- **Context clues** are the words, phrases, and sentences around an unfamiliar word. They can help you understand the meaning of the unfamiliar word.

- You can also use your own knowledge to help you figure out a new word. Read these lines: "Her winter boots have hobnails/Of ice from heel to toe." You know what nails are. What would nails on the bottom of a winter boot be used for? Maybe they would keep a person from slipping.

24 "How it clatters along the roofs,/Like the *tramp* of hoofs . . . ." What does the word *tramp* mean in this poem?

Ⓕ hobo   **Incorrect.** *Hobo* is another word for *tramp*. But that is not how the word is used in this sentence.

Ⓖ dance   **Incorrect.** Replace the word *tramp* with *dance*. It does not make sense.

Ⓗ stomp   **Correct.** The poet tells you that the rain "clatters like the tramp of hoofs." Think about how hoofs sound. The word makes sense in the sentence.

Ⓙ swing   **Incorrect.** Replace *tramp* with *swing*. The sentence does not make sense.

TRY IT! Circle the word or phrase in the lines that defines the underlined word. Then write a definition for the word.

1. "After the dust and heat,

In the broad and <u>fiery</u> street."

_____

2. "How it <u>gushes</u> and struggles out

From the throat of the overflowing spout!"

_____

PRACTICE **Using Context Clues**

Context clues are the words and phrases that surround an unfamiliar word. Sometimes the clues might be right next to the unfamiliar word, but other times you may need to look farther ahead to find them.

Read the following excerpt from a poem. Look for clues to help you understand the meaning of each of the underlined words. The clues may not be right next to the underlined words.

from *The Storm*
by Winston Blodgett

The sky grows e'er <u>crepuscular</u>
Though it is only noon.
And creatures weak and muscular
Take shelter in the gloom.

A <u>ululating</u> wind attacks
My ears from all about.
And home I <u>hie</u> in rapid strides
To shut the howling out.

Read the clues and write the meaning of the underlined words below.

1. **crepuscular:** _____

   Clues: only noon, gloom

2. **ululating:** _____

   Clues: attacks my ears, howling

3. **hie:** _____

   Clues: in rapid strides

B

Teotihuacán: City of the Gods

Probably the best-known pyramids are those in Egypt. However, if you travel about 30 miles northeast of Mexico City, you will find Teotihuacán (tay-oh-tee-wuh-KAHN), an ancient city containing many spectacular pyramids. *Teotihuacán* means "city of the gods." It was given this name by the Aztecs, a later Native American civilization, several hundred years after the city's fall. The Aztecs believed that only the gods could have built the massive structures that line the city's roads.

View of Teotihuacán

Scientists believe that the great civilization of Teotihuacán began about 200 B.C. The city was a religious, commercial, and cultural center that had a great influence on other civilizations for almost 1,000 years. At the height of the city's development, more than 100,000 people lived within its borders. It was not only the largest city in the Americas but one of the largest cities of the ancient world.

Teotihuacán was planned in a grid system that covered about eight square miles. The city has four important landmarks—the Avenue of the Dead, the Pyramid of the Sun, the Pyramid of the Moon, and the Pyramid of the Feathered Serpent.

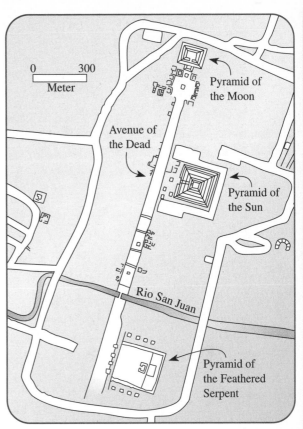

Map of Teotihuacán

Running through the center of the city is the Avenue of the Dead. The three-mile-long avenue varies in width from 40 to 95 yards. On both sides of the avenue are the major pyramids, palaces, and temples. It is thought that the builders of these structures placed them according to the positions of the sun, the moon, and the planets. Stone apartment compounds in the shape of pyramids also lined the avenue. Many families could live in these buildings, which were decorated with paintings, murals, and stone sculptures. These decorations are among the most beautiful of the ancient world. Running underneath the avenue was a drainage channel, it collected rainwater from neighboring streets and carried it to the San Juan River.

The Pyramid of the Sun, a massive pyramid, dominates the skyline of Teotihuacán. It is one of the largest structures ever built by Native Americans. Located on the east side of the Avenue of the Dead, the pyramid is 210 feet tall. Each of the four sides of its base

Go On ➡

B

Carving from the Pyramid of the Feathered Serpent

measures almost 700 feet in length. During excavation, a cave was discovered under the pyramid. It is thought that the cave may have been used for religious rituals.

At the northern end of the Avenue of the Dead is the Pyramid of the Moon. The pyramid was the site of religious ceremonies. Its top lined up exactly with the top of the mountain behind it. The ancient people who lived in Teotihuacán believed that pyramids represented sacred mountains.

The Pyramid of the Feathered Serpent lies in the southeastern end of the city. It is the most striking of all the pyramids. It sides are decorated with carvings of sacred images and more than 350 sculpted heads. Over half of these sculptures depict serpents with feathered headdresses. Because of the large number of graves found at this site, scientists believe the pyramid was used for sacrificial burials.

Unfortunately, the people of Teotihuacán did not have a writing system, so they left no written records. It is difficult to know what a typical day in that city was like. However, judging from the remains of the city, it is clear that many people were master artisans and craftspeople. This can be seen from the sculptures, murals, paintings, and ceramics they left behind. The remains of a large marketplace are evidence that the city was also a major trading center for the region. More than half the population were farmers. Each day they would leave Teotihuacán to work in the fields surrounding the city.

Though scientists know much about the city and its people, much about what life there was like is still a mystery. Just as puzzling is the city's sudden end. About 700 A.D., people stopped living in the city. No one knows for sure why they left or what happened to them. There is evidence that a great fire raged through the city at about this time. Some scientists believe that an invading army started the fire. Whatever the cause, the city and its people never recovered.

Today, scientists continue to excavate the ruins and study their findings. Slowly, they are finding pieces to this mystery. Maybe one day we will be able to understand fully this ancient people and their magnificent city.

Go On ➡

Ceremonial mask from Teotihuacán

STRATEGIES AND TIPS Identifying Author's Purpose

- The **author's purpose** is the reason an author has for writing. The purpose may be to *entertain*, *persuade* or *convince*, *inform*, *explain*, or *describe* something or someone to the reader. In "Teotihuacán: City of the Gods," the author describes the ancient city of Teotihuacán.

- Knowing the author's purpose for writing can help you better understand what you are reading.

25 **What is the author's purpose in writing this article?**

Ⓐ to persuade the reader to visit Mexico

Incorrect. The author does not try to persuade the reader to visit Mexico.

Ⓑ to describe the city of Teotihuacán

Correct. The article describes important features and details about Teotihuacán.

Ⓒ to describe the Egyptian pyramids

Incorrect. The author does not describe the Egyptian pyramids.

Ⓓ to explain the importance of Aztec art

Incorrect. The author does not mention Aztec art.

TRY IT! The author's purpose is to describe the city of Teotihuacán. Look at the map and photographs in this article. Skim the article for details about the city. Then write four things about Teotihuacán that you learned from reading the article.

1. _____

2. _____

3. _____

4. _____

INSTRUCTION FOR TEOTIHUACÁN: CITY OF THE GODS

B

© 2004 Options Publishing, Inc.

 **PRACTICE** **Identifying Author's Purpose**

The most common purposes for writing are to *entertain, persuade, inform, explain,* or *describe.* Knowing the **author's purpose** for writing an article can help you focus on what is important. An author may have more than one purpose for writing.

Sometimes an author can have more than one purpose for writing. Read this article. Think about the author's purpose.

A Rain Forest Adventure

The rain forest is a unique and beautiful habitat. At ground level, there is not much to see. Most of the plants and animals of the rain forest live in the trees, high above the forest floor.

The branches of the very tall trees in a rain forest interlock to form a canopy, or umbrella. On one single branch you can see vines, orchids, and large leafy plants called bromeliads (broh-MEE-lee-adz). The leaves of the bromeliad collect rainwater. One single plant can hold more than 10 gallons of water. The bromeliad is home to tree frogs that live among its leaves and lay eggs in its water.

Sloths move slowly through the canopy. Noisy monkeys make their way from branch to branch. Birds are everywhere. But there are dangers, too. Poisonous insects and snakes also make their home in the canopy. If you visit the rain forest, be careful where you step and where you place your hands. That vine you grab onto may be a green snake!

What are the author's two purposes for writing this article?

1. _____

2. _____

Question 26 This question is about **identifying genre**.

STRATEGIES AND TIPS Identifying Genre

- **Genre** is the type of literature you read.

- *Fiction* is writing that tells about characters, places, and events that are not real. *Myths, folktales, fables, short stories,* and *novels* are fiction genres.

- *Nonfiction* is writing that gives you facts about real people, places, events, and things. *Articles, essays, biographies,* and *autobiographies* are nonfiction genres. The author of "Teotihuacán: City of the Gods" provides facts about a real place.

26 **You can tell that "Teotihuacán: City of the Gods" is a nonfiction article because**

Ⓕ	it is about made-up characters and events.	**Incorrect.** The article provides facts.
Ⓖ	it teaches a lesson about ancient people.	**Incorrect.** The article tells about an ancient people, but it does not teach a lesson.
Ⓗ	it gives facts and information about a real place.	**Correct.** The article gives facts about an ancient city and the people that lived there long ago.
Ⓙ	it is about the past.	**Incorrect.** This does not necessarily tell you that it is nonfiction. Stories and novels can also be about the past.

TRY IT! Skim "Teotihuacán: City of the Gods." Find two facts that help you tell that this work is nonfiction. Write them on the lines.

Fact 1: _____

Fact 2: _____

B

 **PRACTICE** Identifying Genre

Genre is the type of literature you read. Nonfiction genres include *articles, essays, biographies,* and other books about real people, places, and events. Fiction genres include *folktales, myths, legends, short stories,* and *books* about people, places, and events that are made up.

Read the following paragraph. As you read, look for clues that will help you identify the genre.

> Wolves communicate in a number of ways. They bark, howl, snarl, and whimper. A wolf whimpers and whines when it meets another wolf. That shows it is friendly. A wolf growls or snarls to show that it is angry. Each wolf has its own howl. It will howl when it wants to find the rest of its family. It will howl to warn other wolves to stay away from its territory.

Fill in the chart. In the top box, write whether the paragraph is fiction or nonfiction. In the boxes below, write three details from the paragraph that support your answer.

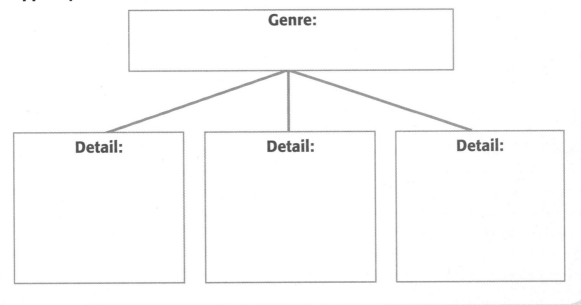

Genre:

Detail: Detail: Detail:

Question 27 This question is about **identifying facts and opinions**.

> ### STRATEGIES AND TIPS Identifying Fact and Opinion
>
> - A **fact** is a statement that can be proved by checking in reference books, such as an encyclopedia or science book. *The ancient city of Teotihuacán is in Mexico.* This is a fact that could be checked by looking at a map or reading an encyclopedia article.
>
> - An **opinion** is a statement that expresses what someone feels or thinks. It cannot be proved or disproved. *A visit to Teotihuacán is the best trip anyone can take.* The speaker may feel this way. Another person, however, may feel differently.

27 **Which of the following statements is an** *opinion*?

Ⓐ	The Pyramid of the Sun is 210 feet tall.	**Incorrect.** This is a fact from paragraph 5. It can be proved.
Ⓑ	Teotihuacán was the trading center of the region.	**Incorrect.** This is also a fact. It can be proved. Skim paragraph 8.
Ⓒ	Running through the center of the city is the Avenue of the Dead.	**Incorrect.** This is a fact. It can be proved. Skim paragraph 4.
Ⓓ	These decorations are among the most beautiful of the ancient world.	**Correct.** This is an opinion. It tells what the author feels about the decorations. It cannot be proved.

> **TRY IT!** **Write *F* for fact or *O* for opinion before each statement below.**
>
> 1. _____ The pyramids at Teotihuacán are the most spectacular in all of North America.
>
> 2. _____ Teotihuacán was planned in a grid system that covered about 8 square miles.
>
> 3. _____ The Pyramid of the Feathered Serpent is the most beautiful pyramid in the city.

Facts can be proved; **opinions** cannot. Articles are often a combination of facts and opinions. When you read, you should recognize the difference between a fact and an opinion. You do not have to accept or agree with an author's opinions.

Read this letter to a local newspaper. Look for facts and opinions as you read. Underline each opinion that you find. Circle each fact. The first one is done for you.

To: The Editor of the Peabody Press

(Last year the city council passed a law that said that dogs had to be leashed.) It is time for our town to enforce the leash law. There are just too many dogs running around. The dogs bark at people and dig up flowerbeds. These dogs are the biggest problem this city has! Last week a group of people went to City Hall to complain about the dogs. Yet, the police still do not enforce that law.

Signed,

Maria Hernandez

Next, read this paragraph. Underline each opinion and circle each fact.

Jane Hannoud is running for mayor. She has been the town treasurer for the last five years. In this role, she has done an excellent job. For the first time in a century, the town has stayed within its budget. There can be no doubt that Jane will be the best mayor ever.

INSTRUCTION FOR TEOTIHUACÁN: CITY OF THE GODS

B

STRATEGIES AND TIPS Identifying Cause and Effect

- A **cause** is the reason why something happens. An **effect** is the result of what happens. You will not always find clue words to signal cause-and-effect relationships. Sometimes you have to infer the causes and effects. To do so, you use information in the article and your own knowledge.

- If you are not sure whether two events have a cause-and-effect relationship, link the two events with the words *because, therefore, since,* or *as a result.* Does your new sentence make sense? If it does, then the two events are a cause and effect.

28 **Scientists do not know much about the people of Teotihuacán because**

Ⓕ	the Aztecs destroyed Teotihuacán.	**Incorrect.** This detail is not in the article.
Ⓖ	they were craftspeople and artisans.	**Incorrect.** This does not explain *why* scientists do not know about the people.
Ⓗ	the city was a trading center.	**Incorrect.** This does not explain *why* scientists don't know about the people.
Ⓙ	the people left no written records.	Correct. Because the people left no written records (cause), scientists do not know much about the people (effect).

TRY IT! Underline the cause and circle the effect in each sentence or pair of sentences. The first one is done for you.

1. Ancient people built pyramids because they believed that the pyramids represented sacred mountains.

2. Because they have found evidence of a great fire, scientists think it was this tragedy that brought the civilization to an end.

3. Scientists want to learn more about the people of Teotihuacán. Therefore, they continue to dig for clues and study their findings.

PRACTICE Identifying Cause and Effect

A **cause** is the reason why something happens. An **effect** is the result of what happens. When you look for cause and effect, think about how one event leads to another. Often, one cause can have several effects.

Read the following paragraph. Think about how one cause can have several effects.

The nine-month drought has created many problems, especially at Madison State Park. Campers are not allowed to have a campfire. Authorities are afraid that even one spark could cause a major forest fire. Without water, many plants and trees have died. There is little food for the animals that live in the park. Madison Brook has dried up, too. It is little more than a trickle of water.

Fill in the chart with three effects the drought caused.

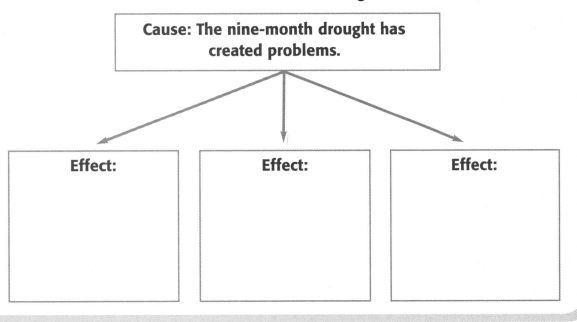

Cause: The nine-month drought has created problems.

Effect:

Effect:

Effect:

STRATEGIES AND TIPS Identifying the Main Idea

- The **main idea** is the most important idea in the article. It tells you *who* or *what* the article is about. *What* is "Teotihuacán: City of the Gods" about? It is about the ruins of an ancient Mexican city.

- Do not confuse details in the article with the main idea. Details give you information about the setting, places, and people in the article. For example, the description of the Pyramid of the Sun gives more information about this landmark, but it is not the main idea.

29 **This article is *mostly* about**

Ⓐ	the ancient city of Teotihuacán and its pyramids.	**Correct.** This is the main idea of the article. Skim the first few paragraphs. The information is all about Teotihuacán and its pyramids.
Ⓑ	the Aztecs.	**Incorrect.** The Aztecs are mentioned briefly in the article, but the Aztecs are not the main idea.
Ⓒ	religious beliefs of ancient people.	**Incorrect.** The article does include some facts about religious beliefs, but this is not the main idea.
Ⓓ	the farmers of Teotihuacán.	**Incorrect.** Farmers are mentioned only as a detail in the article. This is not the main idea.

TRY IT! The main idea of "Teotihuacán: City of the Gods" is to describe the ancient Mexican city and the people who lived there. Write another title for this article based on the main idea.

Title: _____

_____

The **main idea** is what an article is mostly about. It is the most important idea in the article. The main idea tells you *who* and *what* the article is about.

Read the following paragraph. Think about who or what the paragraph is about.

> Want to be a newspaper reporter? It's hard work. A reporter's day begins early in the morning. The reporter needs to find out if any big event happened while he or she was sleeping. Reporters watch newscasts, read the newspapers, and check the Internet. They need to find a story to report. When they do find one, they need to research it. They go to the scene of the story. They interview people. They gather as much information as they can. Then, they write the story and finish it before the newspaper deadline. No one wants to read old news!

Underline the sentence that best states the main idea of the paragraph.

1. Checking the Internet is an important part of a reporter's job.

2. News stories have to be done in a hurry.

3. Newpaper reporting is a demanding job.

4. Reporters must carefully research their stories.

Write a title for this paragraph.

_____

Question 30 This question is about **identifying supporting details** in an article.

STRATEGIES AND TIPS Identifying Supporting Details

- **Supporting details** build on or support the main idea of an article, a section of an article, or a paragraph. The author makes the main idea clearer by supporting it with details.

- In "Teotihuacán: City of the Gods," the author describes the pyramids in the city. These details help the reader form a picture of what the magnificent city might have looked like.

---

30 **Which detail from the article *best* supports the main idea of the article?**

Ⓕ Scientists continue to excavate the ruins and study their findings.

Incorrect. This detail is about the scientists who study the city. It does not support the main idea.

Ⓖ About 700 A.D., people stopped living in the city.

Incorrect. This is a minor detail from the article. It does not build on or support the main idea.

Ⓗ The Pyramid of the Sun dominates the skyline of Teotihuacán.

Correct. This detail best supports the main idea. It adds information about the magnificence of Teotihuacán.

Ⓙ The best-known pyramids are found in Egypt.

Incorrect. The article mentions Egyptian pyramids, but this is a minor detail that does not relate to Teotihuacán.

TRY IT! The people of Teotihuacán worked as craftspeople, traders, or farmers. Skim the article. Find three details that support this idea. Write them on the lines.

1. _____

2. _____

3. _____

Authors use **supporting details** to give more information about the main idea. Supporting details help the reader understand the main idea better.

Read the following article. Look for details that support the main idea.

Building a bookcase may not be as hard as you think if you've never built one. The important thing is to make sure it is sturdy. You can always paint or stain it to cover small mistakes, but you can't hide a shaky construction.

Use boards thick enough to hold the weight of your books. Don't plan for shelves so wide that they will buckle in the middle. Make sure that your boards aren't warped and that they are sawed evenly. When you put two boards together, be sure to use your carpenter's square in order to avoid attaching them crookedly. Apply strong wood glue and hammer in nails that sink into the receiving board at least one quarter of an inch. Attaching the finished bookcase to a wall will help give it more support.

Remembering these simple rules will help you get a good start. The rest is up to you.

Look at the main idea of the article. Write three details that support it.

Main Idea:	When building a bookcase, it is important to make it sturdy.
Detail:	
Detail:	
Detail:	

B

Question 31 This question is about **making inferences**.

STRATEGIES AND TIPS Making Inferences

- When you **make inferences,** you use information in the article, along with your own knowledge to make logical guesses.

- Based on information in the article, you know that about 100,000 people lived in Teotihuacán. Using this information and your own knowledge about how people raise crops for food, you can make an inference. You could infer that the farmers would have needed to grow a lot of food to feed everyone in the huge city.

31 **From the article, you can infer, or guess, that Teotihuacán**

Ⓐ was supported by taxes on its people. | **Incorrect.** There are no details in the article that suggest the people had to pay taxes.

Ⓑ was a small village. | **Incorrect.** Many details in the article suggest that Teotihuacán was a large city.

Ⓒ did not have water to put out fires. | **Incorrect.** There are no details in the article to suggest that this is true.

Ⓓ was a well-developed, prosperous city. | **Correct.** Using the details in the article and what you know about cities, you could infer that Teotihuacán was a well-developed, prosperous city.

TRY IT! List two details from the story that support this inference: *Teotihuacán was a well-developed, prosperous city.*

Detail 1: _____

Detail 2: _____

B

PRACTICE Making Inferences

As you read, you may need to use information in an article and your own knowledge to **make inferences,** or logical guesses.

Read the following short article.

How Not to Go Camping

Whoever said that camping would be an adventure didn't quite mean it the way it turned out on our scout troop's first trip. Here are some simple tips I learned.

1. If you intend to do any cooking, bring matches.

2. Make sure you listen to the weather report the day you plan to leave, or at least the night before.

3. Always check a secondhand tent for holes.

4. Bring waterproof clothing.

5. Don't leave your food where bears and raccoons can get it.

6. Don't rely on the sun for directions.

List two inferences that you can make about the author's camping trip. For each one, write one detail that led you to make that inference.

Inference: _____

Detail: _____

Inference: _____

Detail: _____

Question 32 This question is about **using context clues**.

STRATEGIES AND TIPS) Using Context Clues

- Sometimes an author gives hints about the meaning of an unfamiliar word in the words, phrases, or sentences around the unfamiliar word. Hints about the meaning of an unfamiliar word are called **context clues**.

- The article states: "Stone apartment compounds also lined the avenue. Many families could live in these buildings." Context clues help you understand that compounds were buildings that consisted of many apartments.

- Try replacing the unfamiliar word in the test sentence with each answer choice. Listen for the word that makes the most sense.

---

32 "The Pyramid of the Sun, a *massive* pyramid, dominates the skyline of Teotihuacán." The word *massive* means

Ⓕ small.	**Incorrect.** Try replacing *massive* with *small*. *Small* does not make sense in this context.
Ⓖ carved.	**Incorrect.** There is no information in the paragraph to suggest that the pyramid was carved.
Ⓗ huge.	**Correct.** The author points out that it "dominates the skyline." *Dominates* means it is large.
Ⓙ painted.	**Incorrect.** Nothing in the paragraph hints that the pyramid was painted.

TRY IT!) Write a sentence about Teotihuacán using the words *drainage channel*. Before you write the sentence, look back at the article to see how these words were used.

_____

_____

_____

B

Context clues are the words and ideas that can be found in sentences surrounding an unfamiliar word. These clues can help you figure out the meaning of the unfamiliar word.

Read the following pairs of sentences. Circle the context clues that help you understand the underlined word. Then write a sentence using the word.

1. Mom was <u>livid</u> when she saw the broken vase. I've never seen her so angry.

_____

_____

2. The sea <u>shimmered</u> as the sunlight danced on its surface. The blue water sparkled as if covered with jewels.

_____

_____

3. The <u>stench</u> was coming from the dog's mouth. We had to brush his teeth to get rid of the horrible smell.

_____

_____

4. When the explorers entered the ancient tomb, they could barely breathe the stale, <u>stagnant</u> air. No breeze from outside had stirred the air for years.

_____

_____

5. The diamonds <u>glistened</u> when the sunlight hit them. Their sparkle was almost too bright to look at.

_____

_____